Family Fun in the Smokies

© 2012 Great Smoky Mountains Association

Edited by Steve Kemp and Kent Cave
Design and Production by Lisa Horstman
Editorial Assistance by Julie Brown, Valerie Polk, and Susan Simpson

1 2 3 4 5 6 7 8 9

ISBN 978-0-937207-69-7
Printed in China

Great Smoky Mountains Association is a nonprofit organization
which supports the educational, scientific, and historical programs of
Great Smoky Mountains National Park. Our publications are an
educational service intended to enhance the public's understanding
and enjoyment of the national park. If you would like to know more
about our publications, memberships, and projects, please contact:

Great Smoky Mountains Association
P. O. Box 130
Gatlinburg, TN 37738
(865) 436-7318
www.SmokiesInformation.org

Family Fun

Fun

in the Smokies

A family-friendly guide to the Great Smoky Mountains

by Katy Koontz

Great Smoky Mountains Association

To my mother, who loved books almost as much as she loved me,
and to my father, who has shared his love for the mountains with me
from the very beginning.

ACKNOWLEDGMENTS

I'd like to thank the Great Smoky Mountains Association and especially Steve Kemp, GSMA Interpretive Products and Services Director, for giving me the opportunity to write this book. Steve, himself a gifted writer and editor, was invaluable throughout the process not only for his knowledge about the park and his professionalism, but also for his warmth and great sense of humor. I also owe a huge debt to Nancy Gray, Great Smoky Mountains National Park information officer, who cheerfully endured my countless questions and always came up with the right answers.

Others who deserve my gratitude include Mike Maslona and Butch McDade, interpretive rangers; Kent Cave, district ranger; Joel Ossoff, concessions manager; Karen Ballentine, education supervisor; Ken Voorhis, director of the Great Smoky Mountains Institute at Tremont; Jennifer Pierce, Emily Guss, and Lisa Free, education technicians; Becky Nichols, park entomologist; Bill Stiver, park biologist; Joe Yarkovich, elk research coordinator; Erik Kreusch, park archaeologist; salamander expert Susan Sachs at the Appalachian Highlands Science Learning Center; monarch expert Wanda DeWaard at Discover Life in America; and all the various rangers who fielded my many miscellaneous questions.

I'm also thankful for the many journalists and authors who have written about the park over the years and whose work provided fabulous background material and innumerable fodder for many of my "Fun Facts."

On a personal note, thanks are in order to Steven, for agreeing to move to Tennessee in the first place; to my daughter Sam, for accompanying me on many hikes and for demonstrating her portable-snowman-building skill in Cades Cove; and to my significant other, Colby, for agreeing to come with me on yet *another* hike and for understanding when I needed to work late yet *again*.

CONTENTS

Chapter 10
Waterfall Hikes & Walks • 115

Chapter 11
Hikes & Walks with a View • 125

Chapter 12
Other Family-Fun Hikes • 133

Chapter 13
Camping • 147

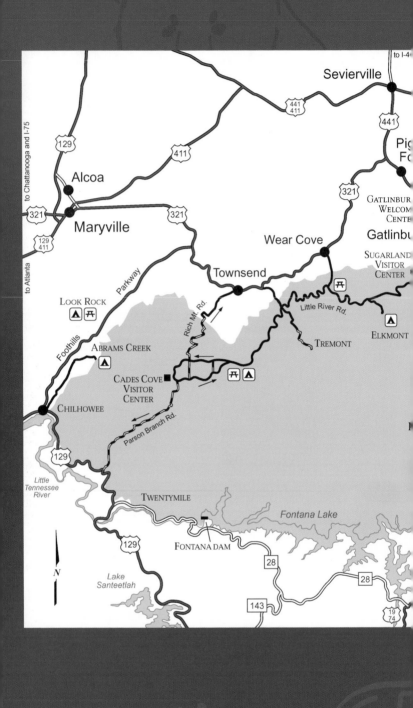

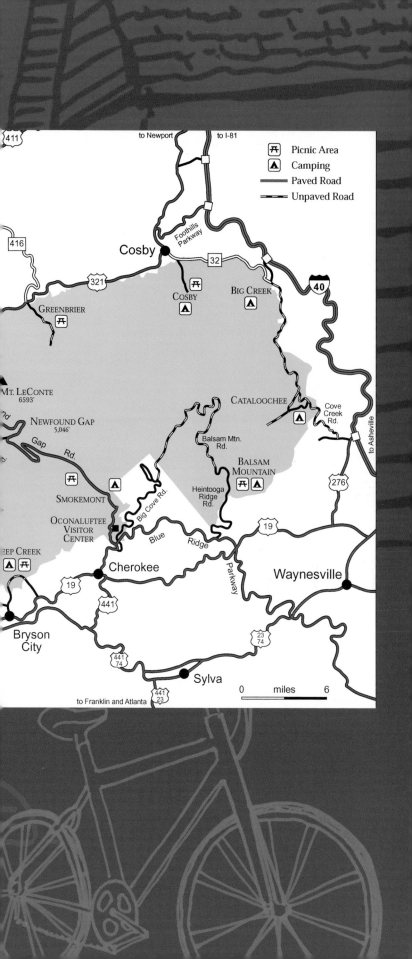

INTRODUCTION

What's So Great About
the Great Smoky Mountains?

It's hardly a secret: The Smokies are special. So special, in fact, that Great Smoky Mountains National Park is the most visited national park in the country. About nine million people come to witness these purple mountain majesties every year.

Part of what makes this park so popular is simple proximity. Sitting astride the Tennessee-North Carolina state line, the park is within 550 miles (a day's drive) of one-third of the American population. And it's free. The Smokies is one of the few national parks that won't charge you an entrance fee—thanks to agreements made shortly after the park was established.

But as compelling as these reasons may be, they're hardly the whole story. People come to the Smokies to see momma black bears with their cubs pawing rotted logs in search of insects. They come to camp in the woods, fish for wild trout, hike high mountain ridges, and stroll on self-guiding nature trails and Quiet Walkways. They come to poke through old log cabins and historic churches, bike past deer-filled meadows, ride horseback through the backcountry, view waterfalls spilling over steep mountainsides, and dabble on sections of the Appalachian Trail.

They come to picnic amidst scads of spring wildflowers, take scores of summer ranger programs, drive on scenic roadways through fiery fall color displays, and marvel at the views in winter when the leaves are off the trees and the snow sparkles on the bare branches.

These outdoor opportunities and more make the Smokies a veritable magnet for families year-round.

Why are the Smokies unique?

Of course, there's the picturesque hazy, bluish water vapor that settles in-between the many layers of rounded mountain peaks, creating the classic Smoky Mountain vista. That view is the reason the Cherokees named the area *Shaconage*, or "Land of the Blue Smoke," long before the European settlers arrived.

FUN fact

There are more than 150 different hiking trails in the national park. Many people have hiked them all. They call themselves members of the "900 Mile Club."

That water vapor comes from abundant rainfall. In fact, the highest peaks in the Smokies actually get enough precipitation to be classified as a temperate rain forest. Even the lowlands get 18 inches more rain every year than Seattle. All that rain feeds some 2,115 miles of rivers and streams, and their countless waterfalls (including one you can actually walk behind).

The water vapor also comes from evaporation from 100 different types of native trees—more species than exist in all of northern Europe. A quarter of the forest is old-growth, with some trees more than 500 years old. Some are more than 20 feet in circumference, qualifying them as some of the largest of their kinds anywhere. This is, after all, one of the largest areas of old-growth forest east of the Mississippi. So when you hike here, often you're hiking among giants, the eldest of which were saplings when Christopher Columbus made his historic voyage.

The abundant rainfall also nurtures more than 1,500 varieties of flowering plants that splash color across the landscape each spring and summer.

Including both plants and animals, the Smokies are home to over 15,000 species—including the iconic black bear, graceful white-tailed deer, majestic elk, playful river otter, and even some critters that exist nowhere else on the planet. The Smokies is, after all, the salamander capital of the world! (Not only are there more species of salamander here than anywhere else, but the park's salamanders easily outweigh all the mammals!) Even the bugs here are showstoppers, including a species of firefly that inexplicably flashes in unison during its mating season each summer.

The Smokies is actually *the most* biologically diverse national park in the continental U.S., and at 800 square miles, it's also the largest federally protected terrestrial ecosystem in the eastern half of the country. Because it's teeming with so much life, the United Nations

declared it an International Biosphere Reserve in 1976.

Why *here?* One reason is the Ice Age, actually. As the mile-thick sheets of ice covered the northern part of the continent more than 10,000 years ago, plant and animal species previously known only in the higher latitudes migrated south for refuge. They found it in the Smokies' rich soil, moderate temperatures, and varied terrain. After the glaciers retreated like a frozen tide, many of the species were already firmly established in various nooks and crannies making up many specific microclimates and ecosystems. So you might say the Smokies was one of the earth's first sanctuaries for endangered species—or even the first popular destination for spring break!

Who lived here before the national park?

European settlers arrived in the Smokies in the late 1700s, at first sharing the land with the Cherokees, who moved into the area about 800 years before them and already had extensive settlements. In the 1830s, the U.S. government forced 15,000 Cherokees in the southeastern states to set out on foot to Oklahoma, a tragic incident known today as the Trail of Tears. A few managed to remain behind, either as legal land

FUN fact

Scientists from around the world (aided by volunteer helpers both young and old) are currently trying to identify every single species of plant and animal that lives in the park—perhaps as many as 50,000 different life forms! The project (called the All Taxa Biodiversity Inventory) began in 1997 and is the largest biodiversity inventory on Earth. In its first 10 years alone, naturalists have discovered more than 6,000 species not known to live in the park before and identified 890 species that no one had ever seen anywhere in the world before (including 74 new kinds of butterflies).

owners or by hiding in the mountains, and today their descendants, the Eastern Band of the Cherokee Nation, live in the 100-square-mile Cherokee reservation that borders the park on its North Carolina side.

Life for the early settlers here was hard, and they lived off the land as best they could. They tilled both fertile and rocky soil and tended crops, they raised livestock, and they hunted, fished, and trapped for food. They built mills to grind grain and later to saw lumber. They erected first log and later clapboard churches in which they both worshiped solemnly and sung rousing hymns. And they built one-room schoolhouses to educate their children during the winter months when they weren't needed to help in the fields.

Mountain life got easier as time went on and modern conveniences became more available. In the early 1900s, the logging industry discovered the Smokies' treasure trove of trees and moved right in. More than a dozen logging camps sprang up as quickly as mushrooms on an old stump. Their names are still used today, including Elkmont, Smokemont, and Tremont. Two billion board feet of lumber came out of these logging camps (enough to build 200,000 modern three-bedroom houses). Many were saddened to see so many mountains cut bare of trees and so the campaign began to turn the Smokies into a national park. It was officially established in 1934. The plundered land was allowed to heal into the rich green forests we see today.

FUN *fact*

The Smoky Mountains were birthed 200 to 300 million years ago (they're 125 million years older than the Rockies), although the oldest rocks found here are a billion years old! Originally, the Smokies were as tall as the Rockies are today, but they've been eroding about two inches every thousand years.

Where did the land for the park come from?

Creating the 22nd national park wasn't easy. While 85 percent of the park's land came from 18 timber and pulpwood companies, the rest was privately owned by 1,200 farmers and 5,000 others who either lived full-time in the mountains or had summer homes here. All in all, some 6,600 tracts of land were stitched together piecemeal like a handmade Appalachian patchwork quilt to form the park.

Funding for all these parcels came from the states of Tennessee and North Carolina, as well as from countless private donors. Contributors ranged from philanthropist John D. Rockefeller, Jr., who gave $5 million in his mother's name, to schoolchildren in nearby Knoxville, who pledged their pennies. (That copper coinage, by the way—with a few nickels, dimes, and quarters tossed in here and there—totaled $1,391.72 in all.)

Understandably, not everyone was eager to leave when the park was established. Several landholders and their families were granted lifetime leases, allowing them to stay on their property (although they could no longer hunt or cut timber) for the rest of their lives. The very last lessee was Kermit Caughron, born in Cades Cove in 1912 as a fifth-generation descendant of the Oliver and Shields families—the earliest settlers here. Caughron lived in the Cove until he died in 1999.

While most national parks strive to erase any sign of man, the Smokies has preserved a slice of its rich and colorful Appalachian culture. Although many structures were razed, more than one hundred homes, mills, schools, barns, outbuildings, and churches remain to tell the story of the mountain farmers who once lived here. You can walk through many of these buildings today, pondering what life was like back then. Consequently, the Smokies (declared a World Heritage Site by the United Nations in 1983) is home to the finest and most complete collection of historic log buildings in the eastern U.S.

FUN *fact*

Fossils found in limestone rocks in Cades Cove are about 450 million years old. The Smokies don't have many fossils, though, because most of the bedrock here was formed before there was much life on Earth.

How do I use this book?

If you're ready to start exploring, first consult Chapter 1 for all the nitty-gritty details you need to know about the park both before you come and while you're here—things like phone numbers and websites, park rules and safety tips, what to bring with you, and even where the bathrooms and vending machines are.

Check out Chapter 2 for suggested itineraries, designed according to the length of your stay. The next two chapters give you good information about the animals and plants you'll encounter, including tips on finding those that interest you most. Chapter 5 gives an introduction to the park's three visitor centers, each of which has its own special flavor.

The bulk of the remaining chapters address all the things your family can see and do in the Smokies, be it taking scenic drives, joining ranger programs or other educational opportunities, picnicking, hiking, camping, biking, horseback riding, or fishing. Pick what appeals most to your family, and flip to that chapter for some stellar suggestions.

The final chapter deals with some educational jewels outside the park that are well worth a stop if you have the opportunity. These sites will add much to your knowledge of the flora and fauna as well as of the cultural history of the area. You'll also find a handy comprehensive geographic index in the back, so wherever your family happens to be in the park at the moment, you can look up what you can do and see in the area.

Sprinkled throughout the book you'll also find fun facts to share with your kids, as well as some fun activities (labeled "Fun Factivities") and simple games and puzzles to keep them occupied.

A personal note

When the Great Smoky Mountains Association asked me to write this book, I was already familiar with many of the places I wanted to include, thanks to having lived in and written about East Tennessee for two decades. But in the year I spent researching and writing this guide, I returned to the scene of the sublime and visited every single place mentioned and hiked every step of each of the hikes and nature trails, specifically with families in mind (and often with my own family in tow). I threw some proposed hikes out, I added some to the list, I quizzed rangers, I chatted with families I met on the trail, and I remembered why I fell in love with the Smokies in the first place.

Mountains, I've found, are a lot like people. Some are rugged, some are mild-mannered, some are old and unforgiving, and some are regal. I won't point any fingers here or name names, but let's just say that the Smokies aren't testosterone-charged, rebellious adolescents out to prove something. They're also not narcissistic celebrities that preen and pose, flaunting their beauty at passers-by. They're more the kindly grandmother or grandfather, filled with character, quick with a story, and guaranteed to be loads of fun. They're the type that when you hug them, they hug you back (and mean it).

CHAPTER I

What Families Need to Know

With a little advanced planning, you'll have everything you need to make a visit to the Smokies both safe and fun. Below, you'll find important phone numbers and websites sharing information about the park, tips on beating the crowds, seasonal highlights and weather, how to find everything from restrooms to cold drinks, important safety tips and park rules and regulations, suggestions for what to bring with you, information on handicapped facilities, seasonal road closures, and driving distances within the park.

Important phone numbers and websites

Emergencies: call 911 or 1-865-436-9171
Note that cell phone reception in the park is generally poor because of the mountainous terrain. While you can sometimes get reception near the park's entrances or on the top of a ridge, it's best not to count on having any cell phone service while you're in the park. If you need help and can't use your cell phone, contact one of the park's employees, who can radio for help.

Visitor information: 1-865-436-1200
This number offers recorded messages about a number of different subjects, including detailed *weather forecasts* (including sunrise and sunset times) and *temporary road closures* that are both updated several time a day, *seasonal events* (including spring wildflower blooms, fall colors, and special events), and information on *camping and overnight lodging,* and *recreational activities.* You can also request an *information packet* or reach the park's *administrative offices* via this number.

Park's website: www.nps.gov/grsm

Park webcams: For a peek at what the park looks like right now, check out:
• **Look Rock** (on the western side looking east):
www.nature.nps.gov/air/webcams/parks/grsmcam/grsmcam.cfm
• **Purchase Knob** (on the eastern side looking northeast):
www.nature.nps.gov/air/webcams/parks/grsmpkcam/grsmpkcam.cfm
• **Gatlinburg looking toward Mt. Le Conte:** www.wbir.com/weather/conditions/skycams/timelapse/smokyMountain.aspx

Park radio: 1610 AM

When you tune in to this frequency at many spots in the park (all marked with road signs), a recorded audio message welcomes you and gives some basic orientation information for that area.

Great Smoky Mountains Association: www.smokiesinformation.org

This nonprofit organization shares information on the park, updated reports on fall colors and spring blooms, and an on-line store offering numerous park guides, books, clothing, and more. You'll find some informative and amusing audio and video blogs here, too. All proceeds are donated to educational, scientific, and historical projects in the park.

How to beat the crowds

The downside to being the most visited national park is that popular areas are crowded at times, creating traffic jams (or "bear jams" when the hold up is caused by the park's unofficial mascot making an appearance).

One way to beat the crowds is to **avoid peak seasons**—mid-June through mid-August and the whole month of October. But with school-age kids, that isn't always practical. The best summer strategy is to **tour crowded places like Cades Cove early in the day**. (Park visitation is heaviest from 10 a.m. to 5 p.m.)

In addition, it's certainly possible to find serene places even in the middle of a beautiful July day. Some of the less crowded areas described in this guide are either the eastern or western parts of the Foothills Parkway (including Abrams Creek Campground and the Look Rock Campground, Picnic Area, and trail to the tower on the western portion); Balsam Mountain off of the Blue Ridge Parkway in North Carolina (including Balsam Mountain Campground and Self-Guiding Nature Trail, Heintooga Picnic Area and Overlook, and the Flat Creek Trail, all closed in winter); Cosby (including Cosby Campground, Picnic Area, and Self-Guiding Nature Trail); Greenbrier (including the Greenbrier Picnic Area and the Porters Creek Trail); Deep Creek, and Cataloochee. See the appropriate chapters for more detailed information on each of these suggestions, including which facilities are closed in winter.

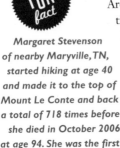

Margaret Stevenson of nearby Maryville, TN, started hiking at age 40 and made it to the top of Mount Le Conte and back a total of 718 times before she died in October 2006 at age 94. She was the first woman to hike all 800 miles of trails in the park (which actually requires hiking 900 miles, since some backtracking is required to cover all the ground).

Seasonal highlights and weather

The Smokies is a four-season destination, with each time of year offering visitors something special. Here's what you can expect when (temperatures are in degrees Fahrenheit and are for the lower elevations, unless specified):

Spring: March high temperatures are generally in the low 60s with low temperatures in the 30s and 40s. Snow can fall any time, especially in the higher elevations. In April highs can get into the 70s, and afternoon showers are common. In May, the highs are in the 70s and 80s, with lows generally in the 40s and 50s.

Wildflower season peaks in April, the month the park hosts its annual **wildflower pilgrimage**. Redbud trees bloom in March, dogwood trees in April, and mountain laurel in May. Bears (and their cubs) emerge from their dens at this time.

Summer: Summers are generally hot and humid, with highs in the 80s and often reaching into the 90s (although the higher elevations are 15-20 degrees cooler). Afternoon rain showers and thunderstorms are common. Evenings are more comfortable, with temperatures in the 60s and 70s.

Summer is when the **synchronous fireflies** show their stuff. More flowers bloom throughout the season, including the rhododendron and azalea, and blackberries and blueberries ripen. The deer give birth to their spotted fawns. The bulk of the park's ranger programs, including special **Junior Ranger activities**, are offered at this time.

Fall: Autumn days start out in the 70s and 80s in September, and fall to the 50s and 60s by November. The first frost generally occurs in late September, and by November the lows approach freezing. It might even snow in the higher elevations. This is the driest season in the Smokies. Rain falls only occasionally.

Fall offers spectacular **leaf colors**, peaking in late October and early November, as well as the **Mountain Life Festival** at the Mountain Farm Museum next to the Oconaluftee Visitor Center. The bull elk start to bugle at Cataloochee, and the monarch migration reaches its peak.

Winter: Winters are moderate in the Smokies, although a lot of snow can fall at the higher elevations. At Newfound Gap, for instance, the annual snowfall can be anywhere from 50 to 75 inches and has topped 100. Yet throughout the winter, the lower elevations rarely see more than a foot of the white stuff all together, usually appearing as a series of dustings that each melt before the next one

Some 150 hiking trails totaling 800 miles criss-cross the Smokies.

appears. Winter highs can sometimes even be into the 70s, although many nights reach the freezing mark.

The crowds are gone in winter, and with the leaves off the trees and better quality visibility, the views are simply super. Waterfalls have higher flows at this time of year, and historic features such as rock walls and the foundations of old homesteads are easier to see while hiking. Biting insects and even snakes lay low in winter, as well.

The very first blooms actually occur now—including the witch-hazel tree in December and the spicebush and red maple trees in February. The **Wilderness Wildlife Week** starts the year off in January with numerous guided hikes and indoor presentations in the neighboring town of Pigeon Forge.

Finding necessities
Restrooms, food, lodging, gas, transportation, & gifts

Restrooms are located at all visitor centers, picnic areas, campgrounds, and riding stables (although be aware that some close in winter). Additionally, you'll find restrooms near Clingmans Dome (closed in winter), and Newfound Gap parking areas, the Great Smoky Mountain Institute at Tremont, Mingus Mill (closed in winter), the Rainbow Falls trailhead (on Cherokee Orchard Road), the Grotto Falls trailhead (on Roaring Fork Motor Nature Trail), Cataloochee, and Le Conte Lodge at the top of Mount Le Conte (closed in winter). Seasonal restrooms are located at the Little Greenbrier Schoolhouse and at the Townsend "Y" (where Little River Road and Laurel Creek Road meet). Some of the horse camps have seasonal pit toilets.

Food and Drinks are scarce in the national park, because of its wilderness character. A seasonal snack bar (open from mid-March

through early November) operates at the camp store at Cades Cove Campground (see the chapter on camping). And those who hike to the top of Mount Le Conte can buy snacks or a bag lunch or (with reservations) have a hot, sit-down lunch at the dining hall. Those who stay overnight at Le Conte Lodge are served breakfast and dinner (and lunch if they are staying more than one night) as part of the fee. (Note that Le Conte Lodge is closed in winter; see the chapter on hikes with a view.)

The Smokies get about nine billion gallons of rain every year!

Otherwise, you'll only be able to eat whatever you bring into the park yourself or what drinks you purchase from a handful of vending machines. You'll find at least some vending machines at Sugarlands Visitor Center, Oconaluftee Visitor Center, Cades Cove Campground, Elkmont Campground (closed in winter), the Great Smoky Mountains Institute at Tremont, and at each of the riding stables (closed in winter).

Drinking fountains are located at all the visitor centers, picnic areas, and campgrounds.

Accommodations in the park itself are rare. The only way to bed down here is to camp (see the chapter on camping) or hike to the top of Mount Le Conte (the shortest trail is five miles) and stay at Le Conte Lodge, which is open seasonally from late March through mid-November. Overnight reservations are required and they go fast. (See the chapter on hikes with a view.)

However, the surrounding gateway communities of Gatlinburg, Pigeon Forge, Sevierville, and Townsend in Tennessee and Cherokee and Bryson City in North Carolina offer a wide variety of accommodations.

Gas stations are non-existent in the park. Fill up before you arrive.

Shuttle busses run between Cherokee, Gatlinburg, and Pigeon Forge four times a day during the summer and less frequently at other times of the year. The Cherokee Trails shuttle (which is not affiliated with the national park) makes a 10-minute sightseeing stop at Newfound Gap during daytime trips. Pick-up locations are at the Cherokee Trails Welcome Center on U.S. 441 near the entrance to the national park in Cherokee, at the Gatlinburg Visitor Center at traffic light #3 in Gatlinburg, and at Patriot Park in Pigeon Forge. Hiker pickups are also available along Newfound Gap Road (U.S. 441) with advance reservations. Call 1-866-388-6071 for a current schedule and rates. Family discounts do apply.

From June through October, the town of Gatlinburg offers **trolley** service (on the tan trolley route) that leaves from the Gatlinburg Mass Transit Center (adjacent to Ripley's Aquarium of the Smokies) and stops at the Sugarlands Visitor Center, the trailhead for the Laurel Falls Trail, and Elkmont Campground before returning to town. Exact change is required. Call 1-800-343-1475 for a current schedule and rates.

Cades Cove Heritage Tours runs guided bus tours of Cades Cove from the Great Smoky Mountains Heritage Center in Townsend. For details, call 1-865-448-8838 or visit www.cadescoveheritagetours.org; (also see the chapter on scenic drives).

Bookstores and gift shops selling a variety of park guides, books on the park, trail maps, t-shirts, hats, toys, local specialty foods, CDs, posters, postcards, mugs, etc. are available at each of the three visitor centers (see Chapter 5), at the Great Smoky Mountain Institute at Tremont, and at the base of the Clingmans Dome Trail. (All purchases from these stores benefit the national park.)

In addition, there's a gift shop next to the bike rental and camp store in Cades Cove Campground, and the Cades Cove and Smokemont riding stables also offer a selection of souvenirs. Finally, you'll find a limited supply of books, trail guides, and gift items at Le Conte Lodge at the top of Mount Le Conte.

Pertinent park rules and safety tips

Water safety: Swift currents, strong undertow in waterfall pools, and hazards hidden beneath the surface make swimming, tubing, and diving dangerous in the Smokies. Drowning is one of the leading causes of death in the park.

Never climb waterfalls; mist and algae make their rocks much more slippery than they may appear. Many people have been killed or seriously injured trying.

When wading or crossing streams, avoid slippery rocks and make sure your footing is good with each step. (A hiking stick helps.) Most of the larger streams in the park cannot be safely crossed without a bridge.

Hiking safety: While hiking, stay on officially maintained trails and keep children in sight at all times. Let the youngest child set the pace, take plenty of breaks (not just to rest, but also to drink water and have a snack to keep energy levels up), and be sure to allow plenty of time to complete your hike before it gets dark. (Sunset is as early as 5 p.m. in winter and as late as 9 p.m. in summer.) A good rule of thumb is that *adult* hikers here cover about 1.5 miles per hour, although you should adjust that pace to reflect your family's level of fitness and the age of your children.

Wear shoes or boots with good ankle support and good traction. To avoid hypothermia, stay dry and avoid wearing cotton clothing in cold weather (synthetics will keep you warmer, especially if you get wet). Always carry plenty of water (more than you think you'll need) and at least some food (such as trail mix or nuts), a trail map, two small flashlights (even during the day), a simple first-aid kit, a wind-resistant jacket, and rain gear. Throw in some moleskin to use in case a blister starts to form—nothing ruins a hike faster than blisters. It's also a good idea to give children whistles for emergency use only (in case they get lost). Let a responsible person know your route. Pack out all your trash—please don't litter.

Drinking water in the park's streams: Even if it looks clear and clean, water from streams can cause illness, so don't drink it. (It's safe if you boil it for at least one minute first or use a water filter capable of removing particles as small as one micron, but that's more trouble than most day hikers care to go through.) Water purification tablets aren't always effective.

Driving safety: Watch the road, not the scenery (use the many pull-offs for that). Winding roads (most notably Little River Road) require careful attention and safe speeds. Be especially watchful of on-

coming motorists who cross the center line while rounding tight curves. Slower vehicles should use pullouts to let others pass.

In winter, roads may be slippery, so leave extra room between vehicles. Also shift to a lower gear (or use L in an automatic transmission) when driving downhill on steep, slick roads to avoid excessive braking, which could cause sliding.

Bicycles: Biking is generally permitted on park roads, but not on most trails or in the backcountry. However, bicycles are allowed on the Gatlinburg Trail, the Oconaluftee River Trail, and on the lower portions of the Deep Creek Trail and the Indian Creek Trail (see the chapter on biking).

Pets: Dogs are permitted in campgrounds, picnic areas, parking areas, and along roads, but only if they are on a leash that's six feet or shorter, or are otherwise restrained. Only two trails in the park permit pets (again, on leashes): the Gatlinburg Trail and the Oconaluftee River Trail (see the chapter on other family-fun hikes). Always pick up pet waste immediately and dispose of it in a trash receptacle. Don't leave pets unattended in any vehicle.

Alcohol: Carrying alcohol in open cans or bottles in your car is prohibited. Alcohol is permitted in campgrounds, picnic areas, and designated backcountry campsites, provided the person possessing the alcohol is age 21 or older.

Picking wildflowers: Picking flowers or digging up plants is prohibited, as is removing anything from the park, including flowers, stones, antlers, etc. You can, however, eat the berries you pick and harvest edible mushrooms for personal consumption.

Feeding wildlife: This is also prohibited and can be dangerous to you and fatal to the animals.

Hunting & fishing: There is no hunting in the park; you can fish with the proper license (see the chapter on fishing).

Bear safety: Seeing a black bear can be the highlight of your Smoky Mountain experience, but remember that bears are wild animals and their behavior is anything but predictable. Although bear attacks are extremely rare, they have happened. Keep your distance at all times and never try to feed, leave food for, touch, or approach a bear.

A good rule is this: If your presence causes the bear to change its behavior (if it stops eating, moves in a different direction, growls, starts watching you, etc.), you're too close.

If a bear approaches, quickly pack up all your belongings and leave the area. Don't run, but slowly back away, keeping an eye on the bear at all times. If the bear follows you, try changing your direction. If the bear persists, stand your ground, talk loudly or shout at it, acting aggressively to try to intimidate it. Move to higher ground so you will appear larger to the bear. Throw rocks at the bear and use a stout stick as a deterrent. Don't run and don't turn your back to the bear. Also, don't leave food for the bear, because this encourages further problems.

Approaching bears closer than 50 yards, or any distance which causes them to change their behavior, is prohibited by law.

Insects: Check yourself and your children carefully after hiking for ticks and chiggers. Beware of yellow jackets, which nest in small holes in the ground or under rocks or logs in all seasons except winter. They are aggressive when they're disturbed, so be careful not to kick any potential nests. Bears looking for larvae to eat frequently dig up yellow jacket nests beside trails in late summer or early fall, so be especially careful at those times. Avoid perfume, powder, and scented

deodorants, which may attract them. If you are allergic, be sure to carry your epinephrine kit.

Snakes: Most snakes in the park aren't poisonous. However, two species (the northern copperhead and the timber rattlesnake) are. Snakes often lay on trails and roads or on rocks in the sun in the late afternoon. Watch where you step and where you put your hands, especially around old buildings and stone walls.

Air pollution alerts: Ground-level ozone pollution (or smog) can be a concern in the park, especially in summer. The Park Service issues advisories when the levels exceed federal standards. When there's an advisory, visitors should either avoid strenuous outdoor activities, like hiking, or at least hike in the lower elevations. Children and the elderly are among those who are more susceptible to ill effects, so monitor them closely.

Roadside assistance: If you need help on the road, look for one of the park's roadside assistance volunteers. They're hard to miss—they cruise around the park in spiffy white Toyota Prius hybrid cars with emergency lights on top and a mountain scene complete with wildflowers and streams emblazoned on the side. These uniformed volunteers carry battery cables and a little gasoline with them, as well as literature such as park maps and brochures. They also have two-way radios to summon help from park rangers and emergency crews. They direct traffic, answer questions, help visitors who lock themselves out of their cars, and otherwise provide all sorts of help where needed.

FUN fact

The smoky blue haze that gives the Smokies its name is thickest on calm, humid, sunny days.

You can also call the park communications center at 1-865-436-1294 or contact a wrecker service in a nearby community such as Gatlinburg, Cherokee, or Townsend.

Car break-ins: Thwart thieves who case parking lots (especially those at trailheads) by always locking your car and taking all valuables with you. Thieves may be watching you as you cover your purse or laptop with a blanket. If you can't take it with you, lock it in your trunk, or better yet, leave it at home.

Handicapped-accessible facilities

The park has a variety of handicapped-friendly facilities. Here's a rundown. (Please see individual chapters for more detailed information, including which facilities are closed in winter.):

Visitor centers: All three of the park's visitor centers (at Cades Cove and Sugarlands in Tennessee and Oconaluftee in North Carolina; see the chapter on visitor centers) and their restrooms are handicapped accessible, all three offer wheelchairs for loan and have accessible drinking fountains. Sugarlands has wheelchair-accessible pay phones. The park film at Sugarlands is captioned for the hearing-impaired.

Historic areas: The Cable Mill historic district (see the chapter on scenic drives) next to the Cades Cove Visitor Center and the Mountain Farm Museum (see the chapter on self-guiding nature trails) next

WHAT TO BRING

- **Dress in layers and always stash rain jackets or ponchos in your car (or backpack).** It can be clear at the lower elevations but raining higher up, and showers sometimes move in quickly. Keep light jackets or sweaters on hand because it can easily be from 10 to 20 degrees cooler at the highest elevations in the park than it is at the base. (For every thousand feet of elevation, you can expect the temperature to drop roughly three degrees.) If you visit in the spring or fall, light gloves and a hat are a very good idea.
- **A complete change of clothes** for each member of the family may come in handy for a number of reasons (or at least an extra pair of socks if you plan to do any splashing about in streams). Wet wipes are also useful for quick cleanups.
- **In summer, bring sunscreen and insect repellant.** The Smokies don't have too many mosquitoes but they do have biting midges and gnats.
- **Bring coolers with food and drinks,** because you won't generally find places to buy food in the park. And fill your gas tank before you enter the park.
- **Bring binoculars** to view wildlife and a magnifying glass for examining bugs and other small objects. Don't forget your camera (and an extra, fully charged battery if you have one).
- **Always keep a park map** (and this guide) in your car for reference.
- **If you're bringing a pet** (see the previous section on pets for regulations), make sure you bring a leash that's six feet or shorter as well as bags to pick up pet waste.

SEASONAL ROAD CLOSURES

Major roads in the park are open year-round, although they are sometimes temporarily closed due to hazardous conditions, especially in bad weather. When there's snow in the higher elevations, Newfound Gap Road (U.S. 441) in particular is often closed. (This happens as often as 20 to 30 times a winter, with the road closing for as little as two hours or possibly overnight or longer.) Restrictions requiring cars to have tire chains or four-wheel drive may also be in effect when roads are snow packed or icy. For updated information on road conditions and closures, call the park information line at 1-865-436-1200.

Secondary roads are often open only seasonally. For exact dates, see the park's website or call the park's information line, although here is the general schedule:

-CADES COVE LOOP ROAD: open year-round from sunrise until sunset, closed to motor vehicles (but not bicycles and pedestrians) on Wednesday and Saturday mornings until 10:00 a.m. from early May through late September.

CLINGMANS DOME ROAD (from Newfound Gap to Clingmans Dome): open April 1 through November 30.

Roaring Fork Motor Nature Trail (from Cherokee Orchard Road near the park's Gatlinburg entrance): open mid-March through November 30. Buses, RVs, and motor homes prohibited.

LITTLE GREENBRIER ROAD (from the Metcalf Bottoms Picnic Area to the Little Greenbrier School): open early March through late December.

PARSON BRANCH ROAD (one-way going south out of Cades Cove): open mid-March through mid-November. Buses, RVs, and motor homes prohibited.

RICH MOUNTAIN ROAD (one-way going north out of Cades Cove to Townsend): open mid-May through mid-November. Buses, RVs, and motor homes prohibited.

HEINTOOGA RIDGE/BALSAM MOUNTAIN ROAD (from the Blue Ridge Parkway and the Cherokee reservation): open mid-May through late October. Buses, RVs, and motor homes prohibited.

ROUND BOTTOM/STRAIGHT FORK ROAD (from the Cherokee reservation): open mid-March through mid-November.

to the Oconaluftee Visitor Center both have paved and/or hard-packed gravel trails that are wheelchair accessible with assistance. Both the Cable Mill building (closed in winter) and the Becky Cable House at the Cable Mill historic district are handicapped accessible.

Mingus Mill (closed in winter; see the chapter on self-guiding nature trails) has a paved and packed-gravel trail that is wheelchair accessible with assistance, as well as handicapped accessible restrooms.

Walking paths and hiking trails: The Sugarlands Valley Self-Guiding Nature Trail—on Newfound Gap Road (U.S. 441)—see the chapter on self-guiding nature trails) is handicapped accessible and also has exhibits designed for visually impaired visitors.

The hiking trails to Laurel Falls (2.6 miles roundtrip; see the chapter on waterfall hikes) on Little River Road and Clingmans Dome (one mile roundtrip; see the chapter on hikes with a view) on Clingmans Dome Road (closed in winter) are paved. But both—especially Clingmans Dome—are very steep and may require some skilled assistance.

The Gatlinburg Trail from the Sugarlands Visitor Center (two miles one-way, or four miles roundtrip) and the Oconaluftee River Trail from the Oconaluftee Visitor Center (1.5 miles one-way, or three miles roundtrip) are both level with hard-packed surfaces that may accommodate some persons using wheelchairs designed for trails. (See the chapter on other family-fun hikes for both.)

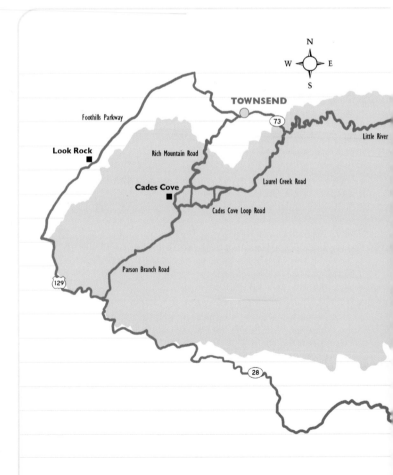

Picnic areas: Handicapped-accessible picnic sites are available at the following picnic areas (see the chapter on picnicking): Metcalf Bottoms and Cades Cove in Tennessee and Collins Creek and Big Creek (where handicapped restrooms are available only during the summer) in North Carolina. The Heintooga Picnic Area (closed in winter) in North Carolina has no handicapped-accessible picnic sites, although

DRIVING DISTANCES WITHIN THE PARK

GATLINBURG TO:
Cherokee: 34 mi
Cades Cove: 27 mi
Newfound Gap: 16 mi
Clingmans Dome: 23 mi
Cataloochee: 65 mi
Greenbrier: 6 mi
Deep Creek: 48 mi

CHEROKEE TO:
Gatlinburg: 34 mi
Cades Cove: 57 mi
Newfound Gap: 18 mi
Clingmans Dome: 25 mi
Cataloochee: 39 mi
Deep Creek: 14 mi

TOWNSEND TO:
Cades Cove: 9 mi
Newfound Gap: 34 mi
Gatlinburg: 22 mi
Cherokee: 52 mi
Look Rock: 18 mi
Cataloochee: 87 mi

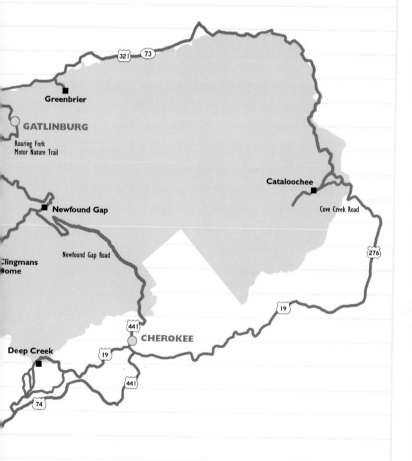

SMOKIES PACKING CHECKLIST

Here is a list of things to be sure to remember to include when you're packing for your trip to the Smokies:

- Rain jackets or ponchos
- Light jackets or sweaters (even in summer)
- Gloves or mittens and hats (light for spring and fall, heavier for winter)
- Bag with complete change of clothes for each family member (to keep in car)
- Sunscreen (for summer)
- Insect repellant (for summer)
- Wet wipes
- Plastic grocery bags to keep trash in until you can find trash cans
- Plastic sandwich bags for safely handling salamanders
- Daypack
- Cooler for lunches, drinks, and snacks
- Binoculars
- Magnifying glass
- Camera (with extra battery and battery charger)
- Leash (six feet or shorter) and bags for pet waste (if you're bringing your dog)
- Whistles (for kids to take hiking in case they get lost)
- Flashlight with extra batteries (in case you get stuck on a trail after sunset)
- Small first aid kit for emergencies

it does have handicapped-accessible bathrooms.

Campgrounds: Five of the park's campgrounds (see the chapter on camping), plus one horse camp, have handicapped-accessible camping sites—level sites that have been modified with paving, specialized tables, and fire grills. They're also adjacent to handicapped-accessible restrooms.

Cades Cove Campground in Tennessee has the most handicapped-accessible facilities. In addition to accessible campsites and restrooms, the camp store here is handicapped accessible, as is a pay phone across the parking lot at the ranger station. There's a paved and level path to the amphitheater, as well.

Other campgrounds with handicapped-accessible camping units include Elkmont and Cosby in Tennessee and Smokemont and Deep Creek in North Carolina. The paths to the amphitheaters at Elkmont and Smokemont campgrounds are paved, although they are a bit steep and wheelchair users may require assistance.

Although Big Creek Campground (closed in winter) does not have accessible sites for the handicapped, the horse camp at Big Creek does.

Horseback riding stables: All the stables in the park can accommodate high-functioning disabled guests for horseback riding, although only the restrooms at Smokemont and Sugarlands riding stables are handicapped accessible. Also, both the hayride and wagon ride offered at the Cades Cove Riding Stables are handicapped accessible.

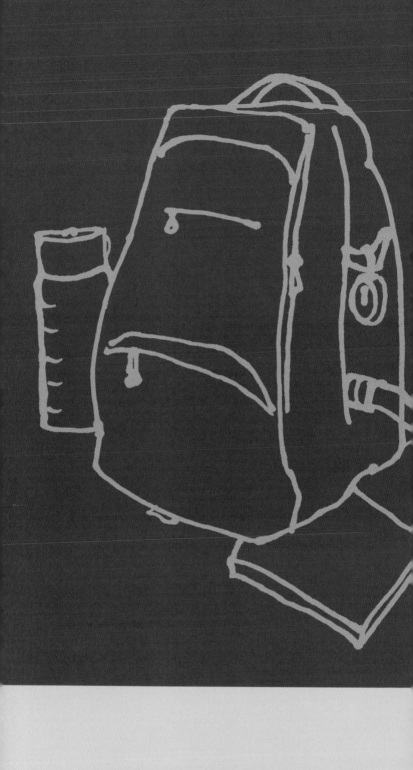

CHAPTER 2

Suggested Itineraries & Activities

You'll find so much to see and do in the Smokies that no matter how long you stay, you'll wish you'd stayed longer. This chapter gives various suggestions for how best to spend your time. Use these itineraries as a guide and feel free to alter them to suit your family's energy level and interests. Do see the individual chapters on visitor centers, hikes, self-guiding nature trails, etc., for a fuller description of what's involved with each option. Also feel free to ask the helpful staff at any of the three visitor centers for additional suggestions and information.

IF YOU HAVE HALF A DAY...

In Tennessee

Waterfall hike: Start at the Sugarlands Visitor Center two miles south of Gatlinburg on Newfound Gap Road (U.S. 441) for a quick trip through the museum and viewing of the film. Then take the short Cataract Falls Trail (0.7 mile roundtrip) from the visitor center or, for a bit more of an adventure, drive west on Little River Road to the trailhead for the Laurel Falls Trail (2.5 miles roundtrip). After your hike, continue west on Little River Road to the Metcalf Bottoms Picnic Area for lunch and to look for salamanders in the adjacent stream.

A gap simply means a low point in a mountain ridge. In other parts of the country, the same thing would be called a pass (in the West) or a notch (in New England).

Mountain vista: Start at the Sugarlands Visitor Center for a quick trip through the museum and viewing of the film. Then take your choice of any of three self-guiding nature trails—Fighting Creek Trail (one mile roundtrip) from the visitor center, or either the Sugarlands Valley or Cove Hardwood trails (0.5 mile and 0.75 mile, respectively, roundtrip) on Newfound Gap Road (U.S. 441). Continue on Newfound Gap Road to Newfound Gap to enjoy the view from the overlook.

History and nature: Start at the Sugarlands Visitor Center for a quick trip through the museum and viewing of the film. Then take the Roaring Fork Motor Nature Trail (closed in winter), stopping to explore as many of the historic buildings as you have time for. You might also want to take the Noah "Bud" Ogle Self-Guiding Nature Trail (0.75 mile roundtrip), located on Cherokee Orchard Road, on the way to Roaring Fork Motor Nature Trail.

In North Carolina

Historic highlights: Start at the Oconaluftee Visitor Center and then visit the adjacent Mountain Farm Museum, with its historic farm and log buildings. Walk the Oconaluftee River Trail (three miles roundtrip) from the farm museum into Cherokee and back, stopping to read the brief displays about Cherokee legends and history along the way.

Mountain views: Start at the Oconaluftee Visitor Center, and then take the Blue Ridge Parkway to Heintooga Ridge Road at the sign for Balsam Mountain. On Heintooga Ridge Road (closed in winter), stop at the Balsam Mountain Campground (closed in winter) to take the Balsam Mountain Self-Guiding Nature Trail (1.5 miles roundtrip). Continue to the end of Heintooga Ridge Road to the Heintooga Picnic Area (closed in winter) to see the overlook and enjoy lunch.

Three waterfalls: From downtown Bryson City, NC, follow the signs toward Deep Creek Campground. Follow the park road past the picnic pavilion to the Deep Creek trailhead at road's end. Hike the Three Waterfalls Loop (2.4 miles roundtrip), which highlights Juney Whank, Indian Creek, and Tom Branch falls. After the morning hike, have lunch at the Deep Creek Picnic Area.

IF YOU HAVE ONE DAY...

For an entire day of Smoky Mountain fun, either combine two of the half-day itineraries above, or try one of the full-day suggestions below.

Exploring Cades Cove: Start at the Sugarlands Visitor Center to see the museum and view the film. Then head west on Little River Road and then south on Laurel Creek Road to Cades Cove, enjoying the cove's 11-mile loop drive. Explore the historic homes along the way, and stop at the Cades Cove Visitor Center to see the historic Cable Mill area. You could enjoy a picnic lunch at Cades Cove Picnic Area (near the camp store) and then go horseback riding at the Cades Cove Riding Stables (closed in winter). If you still have time, park at the Cades Cove Campground and follow the signs to the Cades Cove Nature Trail (0.5 mile roundtrip), in section C.

Another option without the horseback riding but adding a longer waterfall hike would be to hike the Abrams Falls Trail (five miles roundtrip) while you're still on the loop drive. Look for the sign for the trailhead before you get to the visitor center.

High-altitude exploration: Start at the Sugarlands Visitor Center to see the museum and view the film. Then drive on Newfound Gap Road (U.S. 441) to Newfound Gap to enjoy the view at the overlook. Take the Clingmans Dome Road (closed in winter) to its end and do the short but

FUN *fact*

Clingmans Dome was named for Civil War Brigadier General and North Carolina Senator Thomas Lanier Clingman. He was the first man to accurately measure the height of the peak, which he did in the 1850s.

steep Clingmans Dome Trail (one mile roundtrip) to the tower. Then take the Forney Ridge Trail from the Clingmans Dome parking lot to Andrews Bald (3.6 miles roundtrip). If there's time on the drive back, take one of the self-guiding nature trails along Newfound Gap Road (U.S. 441)—either the Cove Hardwood (located in Chimneys Picnic Area) or the Sugarlands Valley trails (0.75 mile or 0.5 mile, respectively, roundtrip).

Both sides of the Smokies: Start at the Oconaluftee Visitor Center and tour the Mountain Farm Museum. Then take Newfound Gap Road (U.S. 441) a half mile to Mingus Mill (closed in winter) and tour the mill. Continue to Newfound Gap and see the overlook. From here, take Clingmans Dome Road (closed in winter) to its end and hike the Clingmans Dome Trail (one mile roundtrip) to the tower. Return to Newfound Gap Road (U.S. 441) and continue to the Sugarlands Visitor Center. Once there, visit the museum and view the film on the park. (You can also do this trip in the other direction.)

Backcountry Exploration: Start at the Sugarlands Visitor Center to see the museum and view the film. Then drive back out through Gatlinburg and take Route 321 along the park boundary to Greenbrier. Either stop and enjoy Greenbrier for a while or continue to Cosby and take the self-guiding nature trail (one mile roundtrip) which begins near the national park picnic area there. Continue on Route 32, crossing over into North Carolina where this very curvy road becomes gravel. Soon after, stop at Big Creek Picnic Area for lunch. Continue on to Cataloochee

FUN fact

The Smokies is one of 40 national parks in the U.S. to be designated as a Climate Friendly Park, meaning it is dedicated to taking action to address global warming. Two big steps the park has taken include making its buildings more energy efficient and reducing emissions by converting all the park's diesel-run maintenance vehicles to biodiesel and using more hybrid vehicles. To find ways to lower your own impact on global warming, check out www.doyourpartparks.org.

A river otter lounges near a stream bank.

in one of two ways. For a quicker trip, take I-40 east to exit 20 and then proceed to Cataloochee. For a more adventurous option, continue on the gravel road from Big Creek all the way to Cataloochee. Once in Cataloochee, take the scenic drive and explore the historic buildings there. Watch for the elk in the meadows by the road at dusk. Return via I-40.

IF YOU HAVE TWO DAYS...

If you have two days to explore, either combine two of the full-day itineraries above, or choose one of the suggestions below.

Hiking, horseback riding, and history: The first day, start at the Sugarlands Visitor Center for the museum and the film. Then go to Sugarlands Riding Stables (closed in winter) for horseback riding. Then drive through Gatlinburg to Cherokee Orchard Road (accessed via Historic Nature Trail/Airport Road at traffic light #8), and on to the Roaring Fork Motor Nature Trail (closed in winter), stopping to explore the historic buildings. Park at the Rainbow Falls trailhead and enjoy the hike to Rainbow Falls (5.5 miles roundtrip). For a different hiking option, continue on Roaring Fork Motor Nature Trail and hike to Grotto Falls (2.4 miles roundtrip).

FUN fact

More than 75 percent of all the medicinal plants that grow in the U.S. today can be found in the southern Appalachians. Botanists call this area "the seed cradle of the continent" because after the Ice Age, much of North America was re-seeded from these plants.

On the second day, take Little River Road west to Metcalf Bottoms Picnic Area. Park here and hike to the Little Greenbrier Schoolhouse (0.6 mile one-way). Explore the schoolhouse and then continue on the Little Brier Gap Trail to the

A family of screech owls nest inside a tree cavity.

Walker sisters' cabin (1.1 miles one-way). Return to Metcalf Bottoms (the total hike will be 3.4 miles roundtrip), and have a picnic lunch. Then continue on Little River Road, which becomes Laurel Creek Road after the Townsend "Y". Take this all the way to Cades Cove and take the Cades Cove Loop Road, exploring the historic buildings along the way. Afterward, take a hayride or a carriage ride from the Cades Cove Riding Stables (closed in winter) at the end of the day to see the wildlife near dusk.

Biking, horseback riding, and vistas: On one of the summer mornings (Wednesdays and Saturdays) when Cades Cove is closed to traffic, rent bikes at the Cades Cove bike rental shop in Cades Cove Campground and ride as much of the loop as you'd like. After biking, go horseback riding at the Cades Cove Riding Stables (closed in winter). Drive on Laurel Creek Road to either the Townsend "Y" or Metcalf Bottoms Picnic Area for lunch. Then continue on Little River Road to the Sugarlands Visitor Center to see the museum and park film.

On the second day, head to the Foothills Parkway west and enjoy the views along this scenic drive. Stop at Look Rock and take the short hike to the Look Rock tower (one mile roundtrip). Have a picnic lunch at the Look Rock Picnic Area (closed in winter). After lunch, stop at the Great Smoky Mountains Heritage Center in Townsend.

North Carolina highlights: Start at the Oconaluftee Visitor Center and tour the Mountain Farm Museum. Then take New-found Gap Road (U.S. 441) to the Smokemont Riding Stables (closed in winter) for a horse-back ride. Continue on Newfound Gap Road (U.S. 441) to the Collins Creek Picnic Area (closed in winter) for lunch. Continue on to New-

FUN *fact*

The highest point in the park is Clingmans Dome at 6,643 feet. (It is the third-highest peak east of the Mississippi.) But the tallest mountain from base to summit is Mount Le Conte (which is more than 5,100 feet tall).

found Gap and enjoy the overlook. On the way back to North Carolina, stop to see Mingus Mill (closed in winter).

On the second day, drive through downtown Bryson City, NC, to the Deep Creek entrance of the park and hike the Three Waterfalls Loop (2.4 miles roundtrip). This fairly easy loop takes in Juney Whank Falls, Tom Branch Falls, and Indian Creek Falls. Afterward, have lunch at the Deep Creek Picnic Area. Then drive to Cherokee and enjoy either the Oconaluftee Village (closed in winter) or the Museum of the Cherokee Indian.

FUN fact

Fontana Dam, on the southwestern boundary of the park, is 480 feet tall—the tallest concrete dam east of the Rockies. The dam produces hydroelectric power and is responsible for the formation of Fontana Lake.

IF YOU HAVE THREE DAYS...

For a three-day adventure, combine some of the previous itineraries, or try the one below.

The best of the Smokies: On the first day, start at the Sugarlands Visitor Center for the museum and the film. Then go to Sugarlands Riding Stables (closed in winter) for horseback riding. Take Little River Road to Metcalf Bottoms Picnic Area for lunch. Continue on Little River Road to Laurel Creek Road and on to Cades Cove. Explore the historic buildings on the Cades Cove Loop Road.

The second day, drive on Newfound Gap Road (U.S. 441) to the trailhead for the Alum Cave Trail. Either hike to Alum Cave Bluffs and back (4.6 miles roundtrip), or continue all the way to the summit of Mount Le Conte (11 miles roundtrip). If you took the shorter hike, follow this with a drive to Newfound Gap to see the overlook.

The third day, take Newfound Gap Road (U.S. 441) to the Oconaluftee Visitor Center (stopping at Newfound Gap to see the overlook if you missed it the previous day). Tour the Mountain Farm Museum. Take the Blue Ridge Parkway to Heintooga Ridge Road (closed in winter) at the sign for Balsam Mountain. Continue to the end of Heintooga Ridge Road to the Heintooga Picnic Area to see the overlook.

FUN fact

Mount Le Conte was named for a teacher. John Le Conte was a professor of chemistry, physics, and natural history who helped determine the mountain's elevation in the 1850s. The older Cherokee name was Walasiyi, which refers to a mythical giant green frog that was said to live there.

Alum Cave Trail.

PLAN YOUR DAYS CHART

Here's a handy chart to help you plan your days in the park. Consult the suggested itineraries and activities in the previous chapter, then read the fuller descriptions in the chapters that follow. Make a plan according to what sounds the most interesting and appropriate for your family. Be sure to ask your kids what they want to do, too!

In the chart below, under each day, fill in the boxes with any specifics you want to explore in each category. For example, if you want to have a picnic lunch on your first day, write in the name of the picnic area you want to visit under the picnic category for day one. If you plan to take a self-guiding nature trail after lunch, pencil in the

	DAY 1	DAY 2
Visitors Centers		
Nature Trails		
Hikes		
Scenic Drives		
Ranger Programs		
Picnic Areas		
Other Activities		

name of the trail under the nature trail category in the same column, and so on. If you plan to go fishing, biking, or horseback riding, fill that in under "other activities." Don't try to fill in every square in every row—just sketch out a general plan for what you most want to do.

Use the Geographic Family-Fun Index at the back of this book to help you find what different options are near each other in the park, and remember to consult the park newspaper for ranger programs and other special activities that are scheduled during your stay. Above all, remember to be flexible (according to the weather, the traffic, and your family's energy level) and always allow for a little serendipity!

DAY 3	DAY 4	DAY 5

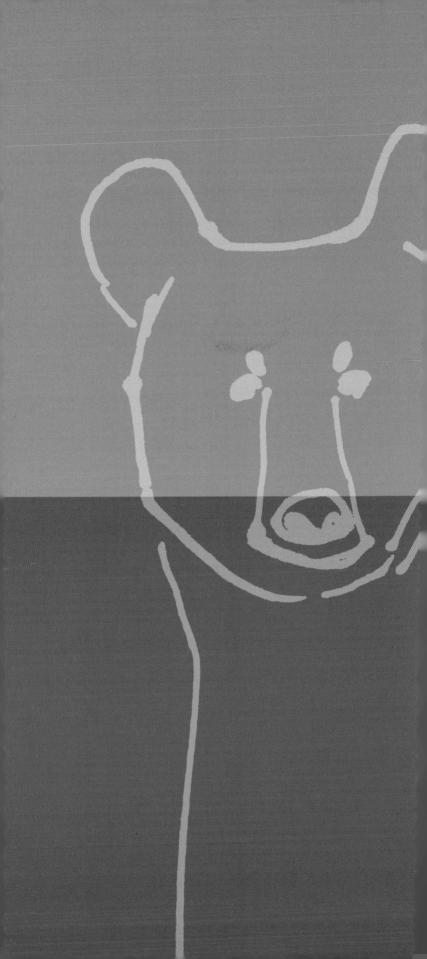

CHAPTER 3

Animals

The Smokies are such a welcoming place to live that more species of plants and animals call these mountains home than any other place in the world between the arctic and the tropics! Experts estimate that 50,000 different life forms exist here, although only 12 percent have been identified so far. Most animal species are the creepy crawly variety, but 66 are mammals, 240 are birds, 50 are fish, 39 are reptiles, and 43 are amphibians. A few are so rare you can find them only here.

At one time, bison and wolves lived in the Smokies.

The following sections give you some background information on some of the more popular critters in the park, along with tips for how best to view them.

General wildlife viewing tips

- **Carry binoculars** (one pair per child, if possible).
- **Open fields** like those in Cades Cove, Oconaluftee, and Cataloochee provide the best opportunities for seeing wildlife, including bear and deer.
- The best time for spotting most wildlife is **early morning or dusk**. Some of the park's species are nocturnal.
- **Some critters freeze when startled**, so even when you don't see movement, look closer and be patient.
- **Watch for smaller animals**, such as raccoons, wild turkeys, foxes, opossum, turtles, and woodchucks (or groundhogs).
- **Winter is great for spotting animals** because the bare trees afford a better view.
- **Enjoy wildlife from a distance.** Do not approach or attempt to feed any wild animal. If your presence causes the animal to change its behavior in any way, you are too close!

Black Bear

About 1,500 black bears, the symbol of the Smokies, live in this park. In fact,

Of the 23 species of snakes living in the park, only two are venomous—the northern copperhead and the timber rattlesnake. For most visitors, the chance of seeing one of them, let alone being bitten, is slight.

An elk shares the road.

the park has one of the highest concentrations of bears in the eastern U.S. (about two bears per square mile). That's six times as many bears as are in Yosemite out West! The best places to spot them are in Cades Cove, Cherokee Orchard Road, Roaring Fork Motor Nature Trail, and Cataloochee Valley, but you can find them just about anywhere.

A typical male weighs 250 pounds (more in the fall, when they can gain three to five pounds in a single day), although some have grown as heavy as 600 pounds. Despite their lumbering gate, they can run up to 30 miles an hour. (The very fastest human Olympic sprinter in the world does the 100-yard dash at around 27 miles per hour.) Bears are also pretty good swimmers—some have even been seen swimming across Fontana Lake! They also love to climb trees, so don't forget to look up every once in a while.

In fact, the bears in the Smokies often like to make their winter dens high above the ground inside hollow trees. Most mothers have two cubs at a time (although they've sometimes been seen with as many as five). The tiny half-pound cubs are born in January, but they don't emerge from their dens until late March or early April.

"Panhandler" bears that dine on garbage and mooch handouts from visitors live only half as long as the average bear. Don't feed the bears (it's illegal, and you could be fined $5,000), and don't leave food where they can find it! Although attacks on humans are rare in the Smokies, those that do happen usually stem from bears going after people's food.

FUN *fact*

Bears do not truly hibernate, although most do sleep for much of the winter. They occasionally leave their den for short periods if they're disturbed (or even during brief spells of warm winter weather). The reason they go into their dens for such long periods is more because food is scarce in the winter than because of the cold.

White-tailed Deer

Although you're virtually guaranteed to see some of the park's 6,000 deer at Cades Cove and Cataloochee, they're also commonly spotted in Deep Creek, Elkmont, Hazel Creek, and Sugarlands. If you hear a loud whistling snort from the woods, especially in the early morning or evening, chances are a deer has seen you (or more likely smelled you) first.

Does give birth in late June, most having two spotted fawns at a time. Look for the bucks to show off during the fall rutting season, when they lock antlers and push each other around to impress the does. Their antlers are most impressive from August through December, but by late winter, they've all fallen off. If you find antlers while hiking, leave them be. Small mammals depend on them as a source of calcium (one of the reasons it's illegal to remove them from a national park).

Elk

Herds of a dozen or more elk commonly grace the open fields of Cataloochee Valley (and sometimes Oconaluftee and Smokemont). Shortly after sunrise and an hour or two before sunset are the best times to spot them, but on cloudy or rainy days, as well as in the winter, they may stay out most of the day.

Elk antlers can grow up to an inch a day and are one of the fastest-growing tissues in the world! The largest rack seen here had nine points on each side. The bulls shed their antlers in March and begin growing new ones right away. They reach full size by August.

Elk mating (or rutting) season is in September and October, when the males are famous for bugling—a sound that starts with a low note and goes high before ending with a few low-toned grunts. You can hear them calling a mile or more away! The calves (usually one per cow) are born from late May through early July. They have spotted coats, similar to fawns, that last until the end of summer.

A successful reintroduction program began in 2001, importing elk from Land Between the Lakes along the Tennessee-Kentucky border and from Elk Island National Park in Alberta, Canada.

Keep an eye out for the Elk Bugle Corps patrolling Cataloochee Valley weekday afternoons and all day on weekends, answering questions and giving informal "elk talks" to visitors. These trained volunteers drive around in special environmentally friendly vehicles.

Salamanders

The park's 31 species of these particular amphibians give the Smokies the distinction of sheltering the most diverse salamander population in the world. They range from the two- to three-inch pygmy salamander to the two-foot-long prehistoric-looking hellbender. One species, the Jordon's red-cheeked salamander, isn't found anywhere else on the planet.

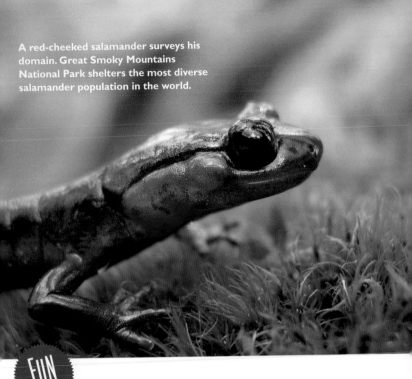

A red-cheeked salamander surveys his domain. Great Smoky Mountains National Park shelters the most diverse salamander population in the world.

FUN *fact*

If you could put all the park's salamanders on one side of a set of beam-balance scales and all the park's mammals (including bears) on the other, the salamanders would weigh more.

Salamanders, although mostly nocturnal, are easy to find—especially in wet weather. The best times to find them are on relatively warm evenings after a rain. Winter is the least favorable season to find them because they burrow deep in the ground. Aquatic salamanders are plentiful in seeps and springs as well as along shallow, rocky streams. Land-based salamanders live in the woods and spend their days resting under rocks, rotting logs, and leaves.

The Fighting Creek and Cove Hardwood self-guiding nature trails (one mile and 0.75 mile roundtrip, respectively; see the chapter on self-guiding nature trails), the area around Mingus Mill (closed in winter; see the chapter on self-guiding nature trails), and the Juney Whank Falls Trail (0.6 mile roundtrip; see the chapter on waterfall hikes) are particularly good spots for salamander sightings, although these amphibians do live all over the park, at every elevation. Be sure to replace any rock or log you turn over to its original position—and don't squish any salamanders when you do!

FUN *fact*

A boy fishing in the Little Pigeon River caught the world's largest hellbender, 29.5 inches long, in 1946. Hellbenders can live to be older than 50.

The natural oils and salt on our skin (not to mention the alcohol in hand sanitizer) is harmful to salamanders because most species here don't have lungs and so breathe through their skin. If you want to pick one up, scoop it gently into a *clean* plastic sandwich bag. (Never use the same bag for two different salamanders to avoid spreading fungal infections.) Don't grab their tails, which sometimes detach; salamanders need the body fat stored there to get through the winter.

Wild turkeys

Wild turkeys are becoming quite common in the park and are most visible in Cades Cove and Cataloochee, although you can also see them around Sugarlands, Greenbrier, and Oconaluftee. You might even hear them gobbling early in the morning. They like open fields on the edge of forestland best, but you can also see them along lower-elevation roadsides, like Little River and Cherokee Orchard roads. April is the peak time to see the males strutting with their feathers all fanned out. In the fall, you can hear them kicking through the leaves in the woods looking for seeds and insects.

The Smokies have 14 different species of fireflies. Only one (Photinus carolinus) is responsible for the fancy flashing pattern.

Synchronous fireflies

The Smokies have become famous for fireflies that flash in unison during their mating season each summer. Typically, the insects flash in short bursts eight to ten times and then all is dark for six seconds. They sometimes blink in waves across a wooded hillside, looking like a string of Christmas lights. The phenomenon is most impressive at Elkmont, but you can see it elsewhere in the park, too. Look for an open area with woods behind it near a stream.

The two-week season begins around mid-June, although it can start as early as late May. The later it gets in the summer, the higher in elevation the famous flashers go. You can even see them as late as early July at the highest elevations. The show generally starts around 10 p.m. and peaks at 11 p.m. By midnight, it's over.

For Elkmont viewing, you must catch the trolley (for a nominal fee) from the Sugarlands Visitor Center, two miles away. (Call 1-865-436-1291 or 1-865-436-1200 for the current schedule and cost.) Elkmont is closed to cars while the trolley runs, except for campers staying in the Elkmont Campground.

Monarch butterflies

Unlike other butterflies, monarchs migrate long distances, sometimes flying as far south as Mexico in the winter. The park's most impressive monarch show is the fall migration, from early August through October. Hundreds of the distinctive orange and black creatures fly together in a cone formation, sometimes covering trees in the higher elevations of the park (like Clingmans Dome and along the Appalachian Trail). Typically, they don't start flying until around 10 or 11 a.m., and they stop when the temperature drops in the early evening.

Monarchs don't flap as much as other butterflies; they glide.

To join a volunteer tagging operation, held five or six days each fall in Cades Cove, call the Great Smoky Mountains Institute at Tremont (at 1-865-448-6709; see the chapter on ranger programs and educational opportunities).

ANIMAL WORD SEARCH

Find the following animals that live in the Smokies. They could be spelled out in any direction—vertically, horizontally, or diagonally. Some are frontward, but others are backward!

black bear
turkey
woodchuck
cub
fox
hawk
monarch

firefly
elk
salamander
millipede
bat
otter
hog

coyote
deer
turtle
rabbit
mice
bobcat
doe

B K H C R A N O M Z S T
Y L C O R A B B I T A U
L N A U S E Y Q G T L R
F K B C H E T O W A A T
E L K A K C H T F C M L
R O W R T B D P O B A E
I K U C U B E O X O N C
F T D E E R D A O B D I
B N E T O Y O C R W E M
M I L L I P E D E L R V

57

CHAPTER 4

Trees, Balds, & Wildflowers

One thing that sets the Smokies apart from other national parks is that its mountains are virtually carpeted with trees—firs, oaks, hickories, maples, beeches, birches, walnuts, pines, ashes, sweetgums, sourwoods, magnolias, and over a hundred others. In addition, the park boasts about the same number of species of shrubs, 1,660 species of flowering plants, and more than 4,000 species of non-flowering plants (like ferns and mosses), many of them rare. It's a veritable greenhouse!

Here's a good way to imagine the variety: If you hiked from the park's lowest elevations to its highest peaks, you'd walk through all the same ecological zones that you'd pass on a trip from Georgia to Maine. As a result, the Smokies' fall colors and spring blooms are real showstoppers.

Trees

The Smokies win the diversity prize for having more species of trees than any other national park in the country. In fact, these mountains contain almost every type of forest that exists in the eastern U.S.—cove hardwood, pine-oak, hemlock, northern hardwood, and spruce-fir. That's a lot of trees! A whopping 80 percent of the park is blanketed with deciduous forests—trees that lose their leaves in the fall. The rest are mostly evergreen trees.

FUN *fact*

The bark of the flowering dogwood tree looks remarkably like snakeskin.

The **cove hardwood forest**, up to 4,500 feet in elevation, has the largest number of tree species in the Smokies (including sugar maple, yellow birch, silverbell, yellow buckeye, and tuliptree). In just one acre, you might find as many as 20 different types of trees and 40 species of wildflowers. To explore this amazingly rich environment, take the **Cove Hardwood Self-Guiding Nature Trail** (0.75 mile roundtrip). The trailhead is located in the Chimneys Picnic Area on Newfound Gap Road (U.S. 441) (see the chapter on self-guiding nature trails).

Although many species of trees in this environment are quite tall, two smaller trees here have particularly lovely blooms—the redbud with its brilliant magenta flowers and the gracefully elegant dogwood,

whose blooms are white. Both splash color with wild abandon across green mountainsides each spring.

The **pine and oak forest** thrives on relatively dry, exposed slopes and ridges up to 3,000 feet, found most often on the park's western side. Some white pines here are taller than 200 feet, which is as tall as a 20-story building! The **eastern hemlock forest** occupies the banks of streams and moist, shady slopes up to 4,000 feet in elevation. The largest eastern hemlock in the U.S. is in the Smokies—its trunk is almost 17 feet in circumference and it's 173 feet tall. Some are over 500 years old. It's not hard to see why some people call eastern hemlocks the "redwoods of the East."

The **northern hardwood forest** is most common at the park's middle to upper elevations, from 3,500 to 5,000 feet. These are the highest elevation deciduous forests in the eastern U.S. and show off yellow birch,

FUN *factivity*

Find some hemlock trees and look closely at the base of their needles. You may see what appear to be small spitballs or pieces of cotton fluff. This is actually an aphid-like insect called the hemlock woolly adelgid that arrived in this country in the 1920s on trees imported from Europe. This destructive little critter first appeared in the park in 2002. (Its cousin, the balsam woolly adelgid, has killed many of the Fraser firs at the park's higher elevations, including Clingmans Dome.) The park is using several different strategies to stop the spread of these insects, including soap sprays, soil treatments, and tiny predator beetles the size of poppy seeds that eat only adelgids. So far, over 100,000 hemlocks have been treated.

American beech, and maple trees. This is where you'll find some excellent leaf colors in early autumn.

Spruce-fir forests cover only about two percent of the park's land, crowning the highest elevations—those above 4,500 feet. This is the land of Fraser fir and red spruce. One way to tell them apart is that the cones on the Fraser firs stand upright on the branches instead of hanging down, the way the cones on red spruce do. Unfortunately, most of the Fraser firs are dying from an insect called the balsam woolly adelgid (pronounced ah-DEL-jid). Up to 50,000 adelgids can infest a single Fraser fir. They actually inject the fir trees with toxins that block the tree from absorbing nutrients, and the stately giants literally starve to death.

Fall colors: The fall colors display is truly spectacular in the Smokies. Look for the most breathtaking displays in years with lots of sunny, clear, and warm autumn days followed by cold nights.

The peak depends on a variety of weather-related factors and is difficult to predict. It also varies with the elevation. The show starts at the higher elevations, usually beginning around mid-September and peaking the first half of October. Good high-elevation drives for fall colors include **Clingmans Dome Road** off of Newfound Gap Road (U.S. 441), the **Blue Ridge Parkway** starting near the Oconaluftee Visitor Center, and the **Foothills Parkway** (both the section by Cosby just north of the park and the western section near Townsend). (See the chapter on scenic drives for descriptions of all of these.)

At the mid- and lower-elevation areas, there are always a few early species that add color to the woods, notably sourwood and blackgum. The peak for maples, birches, hickories, and oaks comes in late October or early November. The trees that live in these elevations have brighter colors than the ones that live higher up. The best drives in this range include the **Roaring Fork Motor Nature Trail** near the Gatlinburg entrance, **Cataloochee** on the eastern edge of the park, and **Little River Road**. (See the chapter on scenic drives for descriptions of all of these.)

Andrews Bald contains a small bog where carnivorous sundew plants grow. These plants are similar to Venus flytraps—they eat insects! The sundew plant's leaves sport sticky hairs that are coated with a liquid that smells good to insects. When an unsuspecting bug lands on a sundew leaf, the tiny critter gets stuck. Then the sundew leaf's sticky hairs wrap around the insect, trapping it, as the plant's digestive juices take over.

Balds

The Smokies are such an old mountain range that some of the mountains are bald (*har-har*)! The summits of several mountains have no trees—just open meadows of natural grasses, wildflowers, and flowering bushes. No one knows for sure how or why these grassy balds formed (they were already here when the pioneers arrived), but lightning, ice storms, insects, animal grazing, windstorms, disease, fire, and Indian occupation have all been suggested at various times. One thing is for certain about them: the panoramic views they offer are astounding. (See the description of Andrews Bald in the chapter on hikes with a view.)

I WONDER WHERE THE FLOWERS ARE?

A rough guide to when and where wildflowers bloom

FLAME AZALEAS (blooms of many different colors, including white, peach, orange, yellow, and red): April and May for the low and mid-elevations (especially pretty along Balsam Mountain Road; see the chapter on scenic drives); late June and early July for Gregory Bald; early July for Andrews Bald, which also boasts three species of orchids and Catawba rhododendron (see the chapter on hikes with a view).

MOUNTAIN LAUREL (both white and pink blooms): early May through June (especially fine along the appropriately named Laurel Falls Trail—see the chapter on waterfall hikes—but can be found along many trails and roadways throughout the park).

CATAWBA RHODODENDRON (rose and purple blooms): early to late June, found only above 3,500 feet (especially pretty along Newfound Gap Road, above the Chimney Tops trailhead, and along the Alum Cave Trail and Andrews Bald—see the chapter on hikes with a view).

ROSEBAY RHODODENDRON (white blooms): June in the lower elevations; July in the mid-elevations (at or below 5,000 feet). These bushes prefer to grow around streams and in ravines and are the most common rhododendron in the park.

Other flowering plants continue to bloom all summer long in the park, as well as through the fall. Good general drives for wildflowers include Little River Road and Roaring Fork Motor Nature Trail (especially at the Noah "Bud" Ogle Place; see the chapter on self-guiding nature trails) in late March and April, Clingmans Dome Road from late April through August, and Heintooga Ridge Road and Balsam Mountain Road on the North Carolina side in May. (See the chapter on scenic drives for descriptions of all of these.) Metcalf Bottoms Picnic Area (see the chapter on picnicking) on Little River Road is another popular spot for blooms.

Yellow-fringed orchids.

The Smokies also have **heath balds** (sometimes called laurel slicks or laurel hells), extremely dense areas of mountain laurel and rhododendron with very few trees. They're especially beautiful when the mountain laurel and rhododendron bloom in summer, appearing from a distance as though someone has flung a giant bucket of purple paint across the mountaintops.

The latest theory about how heath balds came to be involves severe fires that raged over a thousand years ago. The plants in these communities make the soil so acidic that it actually keeps trees from growing.

Wildflowers

Some Smoky Mountain wildflowers actually bloom as early as March, while some bloom as late as November.

All the rain that falls in the mountains, the Smokies' relatively mild climate, and all of its diverse ecosystems mean at least one thing in the spring: tons of wildflowers everywhere. The Smokies is decked out regally in blooms of every color.

Although as with the fall colors, the peak is impossible to predict, the season generally starts with what are called ephemeral (short-lived) wildflowers that peak in early to mid-April (although blooms begin as early as late March in the lower elevations). These brightly

63

colored beauties, which usually last until about mid-May, happily dot the forest floor before the trees have a chance to leaf out and block the sunlight.

Then, from about mid-May to mid-July, the mountain laurel, rhododendron, and azalea bushes take their turn, with big, bold blooms adorning the thick green tangle.

Probably the best general wildflower walk in the park is the **Cove Hardwood Self-Guiding Nature Trail** (see the chapter on self-guiding nature trails), especially famous for its large white trillium. But by mid-April, it's hard to pick a bad trail for wildflowers in the lower elevations.

Some other excellent wildflower trails described in the hiking chapters of this guide include the **Cosby and Elkmont self-guiding nature trails** (see the chapter on self-guiding nature trails); the **Rainbow Falls, Grotto Falls, Hen Wallow Falls, and Abrams Falls trails** (see the chapter on waterfall hikes); the **Oconaluftee River Trail** near the Cherokee entrance; the **Porters Creek Trail** near the Greenbrier entrance (especially from March through April); the **Middle Prong Trail** in the Tremont area; and the section of the **Appalachian Trail** between Newfound Gap and Road Prong Trail (from mid-April through May). (See the chapter on other family-fun hikes for descriptions of all of these.)

FUN *fact*

The Annual Spring Wildflower Pilgrimage in April offers a week's worth of guided hikes, walks, photo tours, art classes, and indoor seminars about the mountain wildflowers in the park, Appalachian cultural history, wildlife ecology, and more. The event, which started in 1951, draws guests from over 30 states. More than 150 programs are available for those who pay a small registration fee. For additional information, visit the event's official website at www.springwildflower pilgrimage.org.

CHAPTER 5

Visitor Centers

The park has three visitor centers (two in Tennessee and one in North Carolina), and each is open every day except Christmas. Rangers staff information desks at Sugarlands and Oconaluftee—the visitor centers at the main park entrance for each state—to help you plan your visit.

Be sure to check out the new three-dimensional maps at Sugarlands and Oconaluftee. These fascinating photographic-topographic maps are great for showing your kids what the park looks like from the air and for letting them see where you plan to go.

In addition, grab one of the free fold-out park maps and a copy of *Smokies Guide*, the quarterly park newspaper chock full of news and information about what's happening at the park during the current season.

In addition to the shops in the park's visitor centers, the nonprofit Great Smoky Mountains Association has several other shops at welcome centers in the communities surrounding the park. You'll find them in downtown Gatlinburg (at traffic light #3), on the spur between Pigeon Forge and Gatlinburg, in Sevierville, and in Townsend.

All three visitor centers have restrooms and water fountains, and they are all handicapped accessible (see individual descriptions in this chapter for more handicapped facilities). Sugarlands and Oconaluftee also have pay phones and vending machines that sell drinks. Cades Cove doesn't have vending machines, but you can buy bottled water and trail snacks in the bookstore/gift shop.

Each visitor center also has an excellent bookstore and gift shop that's run by the nonprofit Great Smoky Mountains Association. These shops stock hiking guides, picture books about the park, cookbooks, junior ranger booklets, story books for children, stuffed animals and other toys, mugs, calendars, posters, post cards, park t-shirts, caps, walking sticks, DVDs, CDs, and more. They also sell a wide variety of specialty foods, including local jams, honey, molasses, and sorghum molasses like the mountain folk made. Often, you can even get a free sample of some of these goodies. (All profits from these shops benefit the park, by the way.)

If you want to mail postcards from the park, the park gift shops all sell stamps. You'll find a mail drop at Sugarlands, near the entrance, and the rangers behind the desk at Oconaluftee will take your stamped mail and post it for you.

Some of the park's many ranger-guided programs begin at the various visitor centers, as well (see the chapter on ranger programs and educational opportunities). What follows is a short description of each of the visitor centers and the various exhibits and other fun things they offer.

SUGARLANDS

LOCATION: Just inside the park boundary near the Gatlinburg, TN, entrance, at the northern end of Newfound Gap Road (U.S. 441).

HOURS: Opens at 8 a.m., year-round. Closes as late as 7 p.m. in the summer and as early as 4:30 p.m. during the winter. (For exact hours, see the park's website.)

HANDICAPPED FACILITIES: Rest rooms, water fountain, phone; wheelchairs available to borrow; film is captioned for hearing-impaired.

Sugarlands is the largest of the park's three visitor centers and offers the most. First, head to the surround-sound theater to watch the free 20-minute color film. It starts every half hour throughout the day. It's very engaging and the cinematography is quite rich. The film covers a lot of ground in a general overview that includes the plants and animals in the park, background on Cherokee history and their legend of how the Smokies were created, the culture of the mountain farmers, the logging industry, how the park was born, the geologic history of the area, as well as the park's current challenges.

FUN *fact*

Sugarlands got its name because of all the sugar maple trees in the area that were used to make maple syrup.

Then tour the museum, which does a great job of packing a lot of natural history exhibits into a relatively small space. Each ecosystem has its own section, so there's one for each type of forest, as well as for balds, wet places, and meadows. Kids will enjoy the realistic models and taxidermied animals for each area. Highlights include the black bear, bobcat, gray fox, great horned owl, wild hog, and various snakes, fish, turtles, and salamanders. Don't miss the giant hellbender! As for the park's plants, you'll see examples here of the

Oconaluftee and Sugarlands
visitor centers have flat-screen
displays giving the current
weather conditions, any road
closure information, and
even the day's sunrise
and sunset times.

popular wildflowers that grow all over the park—not to mention plants like poison ivy! (This gives you an excellent itch-free opportunity to teach your kids how to recognize this vexing vine!)

Behind the visitor center is the start of the **Fighting Creek Self-Guiding Nature Trail** (one mile roundtrip; see the chapter on self-guiding nature trails) and the trail to **Cataract Falls** (0.7 mile roundtrip). The **Gatlinburg Trail** (two miles one-way, or four miles roundtrip) also begins behind the visitor center.

CADES COVE

LOCATION: Near the mid-point of the 11-mile, one-way Cades Cove Loop Road.

HOURS: Opens at 9 a.m., year-round. Closes as late as 7:30 p.m. in the summer and as early as 4:30 p.m. during the winter. (For exact hours see the park's website.)

HANDICAPPED FACILITIES: Rest rooms, water fountain; wheelchairs available to borrow.

The Cades Cove Visitor Center is a small log cabin that houses a bookstore and gift shop. Park rangers, volunteers, and craftspeople lead a number of walks, talks, and demonstrations, mostly during summer and fall.

Set off down the path outside the visitor center to explore the many different buildings in this little historic area, all except the mill brought here from other places in the park. (The trail here is level and surfaced with hard-packed gravel, making it handicapped-accessible.)

The walk begins with a **blacksmith shop** (built in modern times by the Park Service to resemble an old-fashioned one), followed by a **cantilever barn**. This odd style of barn looks a little bit like a muffin, because the second story is larger than the first and hangs over it.

FUN *fact*

Although the Cable Mill was built with a capacity to grind 150 pounds of meal an hour, today it usually grinds only five to six pounds in the same amount of time.

The John P. Cable gristmill and its large, moss-covered waterwheel is next, although you might want to first follow the wooden flume to the little dam and the pond that supplies the mill with water. The mill was built in 1868 and still operates (from mid-March through late November). Walk inside to see a handful of exhibits and to hear the miller explain how the mill works. You can even buy a bag of flour or cornmeal like those that were ground here. (The mill is handicapped accessible.)

After the mill, you'll pass a **smokehouse**, followed by the **Gregg-Cable home**—probably the first house in the cove that was built with frame lumber instead of logs. Dating from 1879, this building was at different times a store and a boarding house as well as a residence. (Ramps here make the house wheelchair-accessible.)

The rest of the historic buildings in this area include a **corncrib** and a **"drive-through" barn** with stalls on either side of a center aisle. On your way back to your car, you'll pass an odd structure in the middle of the grass. It's a **sorghum mill** for making molasses.

After the farmers harvested the sorghum stalks in the fall and

stripped off the leaves, they fed them through the rollers of this mill. To make the rollers turn, they hitched a horse or mule to the long wooden pole and led it around in a circle. The rollers pressed out the sugary juice, which the family collected and then boiled in the big metal pans (called a sorghum furnace) that you see nearby, until it became sorghum molasses. Sorghum molasses is not the same as regular molasses made from sugar cane, but it's used much the same way as a sweetener. If you want to try it, you can buy some in any of the gift shops.

Becky Cable (who was born in 1844 and moved to Cades Cove in 1868) was the last to live in the Gregg-Cable house. She never married, but when her brother got sick, she raised his brood of children, worked as a miller, ran a boarding house, spun wool, cooked and sewed, plowed and planted the fields, and herded cattle on her 600-acre farm. She lived to be 96 and died in 1940, after the park was established.

OCONALUFTEE

LOCATION: Just inside the park boundary near the Cherokee, NC, entrance, at the southern end of Newfound Gap Road (U.S. 441).

HOURS: Opens at 8 a.m. and closes as late as 7 p.m. in the summer and as early as 4:30 p.m. during the winter. (For exact hours, see the park's website.)

HANDICAPPED FACILITIES: Rest rooms, phone; wheelchairs available to borrow.

FUN factivity

Though not a full-fledged visitor center, Clingmans Dome Information Center has exhibits, staff to answer your questions, and books, maps, water, snacks, jackets, and other provisions. It is located in the handsome Civilian Conservation Corps (CCC)-built stone building at the start of the trail to Clingmans Dome tower.

The new **Oconaluftee Visitor Center and Museum** was completed here in 2011. Cultural exhibits in the new center give an overview of the people who lived in the Smokies before it became a national park (including the Cherokee and the European settlers) as well as of industries such as logging and milling. The Civilian Conservation Corps (CCC) built the old visitor center as an administration building in 1940.

The adjacent **Mountain Farm Museum** displays an interesting group of historic buildings and is described in the chapter on self-guiding nature trails. This is also the beginning of the **Oconaluftee River Trail** (three miles roundtrip), which follows the Oconaluftee River to downtown Cherokee (see the chapter on other family-fun hikes).

I SPY SOMETHING...

To play I Spy, one person starts out selecting an object that they can see from where they are, noting something distinctive about it. Then the person says, "I spy something _____ (mentioning what the distinctive quality is). What is it?" Then each other person in the family takes turns trying to guess what the object is. The first person to guess correctly gets to select the next object for everyone else to guess.

For example, if you select a leaf, you might say, "I spy something green. What is it?" If you select an ant, you might say, "I spy something crawling. What is it?" Or if you select a crow, you might say, "I spy something black that is flying. What is it?" See how many different things your whole family can guess.

CHAPTER 6

Scenic Drives

The scenic drives in the Smokies can introduce you to plenty of wildlife, rushing streams, colorful flowers, lush forests, mountain vistas, and historic buildings—all from the seat of your car. To get the full flavor of the Smokies, be sure to park in plenty of the many pulloffs so you can get out and explore on foot, as well. Please don't restrict your Smoky Mountain experience to asphalt alone. He who enters and exits this park without putting sneaker to earth is missing much. Nonetheless, several scenic drives provide an excellent introduction to this park—not to mention a bit of a break for tiny tired feet.

The park has more than 270 miles of roadways including both paved roads as well as gravel and dirt backcountry byways, all fairly easy for most cars to negotiate. (Gravel roadways may be a little bumpy, but do not require four-wheel-drive vehicles. However, it's recommended that RVs, vehicles pulling trailers, and busses not use gravel back roads.) Most back roads do close in the winter (see the chapter on what families need to know), so plan accordingly.

FUN fact

Driving to Newfound Gap from the Sugarlands Visitor Center, you'll pass through two tunnels along the way.

The lay of the land is simple—you'll find only two main road systems. Newfound Gap Road (U.S. 441) crosses the mountains and connects the Sugarlands and Oconaluftee visitor centers. Little River and Laurel Creek roads run end-to-end and together connect Sugarlands with Cades Cove. In addition, the park has several smaller dead-end segments, loops, and less trafficked unpaved roads, leading to campgrounds, picnic areas, historic sites, and trailheads offering out-of-the-way treasures well worth exploring.

Here are quick descriptions of the park's best scenic drives. Note that the first four (Newfound Gap Road, Cades Cove Loop Road, Roaring Fork Motor Nature Trail, and the Cataloochee Auto Tour) have their own detailed auto tour booklets that give much more information and are keyed to the numbered posts you will see along the way. These booklets are available for sale at a nominal price at the visitor centers or on the honor system from dispensers at the start of most of these roads.

Audio tours of Newfound Gap Road (U.S. 441) are also available online from the website of the Great Smoky Mountains Association (www.smokiesinformation.org). The association also publishes the book *The Smokies Road Guide*, another great resource available for sale online as well as in the park's gift shops.

Newfound Gap Road (U.S. 441)

FUN
fact

Most families drive only half of this 29-mile road, usually from one end of the park to the overlook at Newfound Gap (5,048 feet in elevation), relatively close to the road's midpoint. From either the Oconaluftee end or the Sugarlands end, the road climbs around 3,000 feet and passes through most of the different types of forest (see the chapter on trees and wildflowers). Ask the kids to watch the trees change as you drive. At the very least, they'll notice that you'll start out surrounded by hardwoods and end up among evergreens. You'll find a number of pull-offs along the way, some for Quiet Walkways (see the chapter on self-guiding nature trails), some for exhibits, and some for overlooks.

The Loop was the road engineers' answer to a steep route without a lot of room for switchbacks. But a famous local mountain guide and all-round colorful character named Wiley Oakley offered a different story. He used to joke that when the road was built, they had some left over, so they tied a knot in it! (Wiley's daughter, Lucinda Ogle, appears at age 93 in a park film at the Sugarland Visitor Center.)

It will definitely be a good bit cooler (and in winter, downright cold) at the top, so be prepared with sweatshirts and coats. Driving the entire 29 miles between the Sugarlands and Oconaluftee visitor centers takes about an hour, one-way, without stops.

Here's what you'll see, coming from each end of the road to Newfound Gap.

From Tennessee toward Newfound Gap: Just past the Sugarlands Visitor Center, you'll find the **Sugarlands Valley Self-Guiding Nature Trail** (0.5 mile roundtrip; see the chapter on self-guiding nature trails). This is a short paved trail (for handicapped access) that you can easily take a stroller on.

The Chimneys Picnic Area (see the chapter on picnicking) is 4.6 miles from the Sugarlands Visitor Center. This is also where you'll find the trailhead for the **Cove-Hardwood Self-Guiding Nature Trail** (0.75 mile roundtrip), especially fabulous in early and mid-April when the wildflowers bloom.

About a mile further on, you can stop at the **Chimney Tops Overlook** to see twin spires rising 2,000 feet, one of the steepest cliffs in the park. The Cherokee thought this unusual formation resembled the base of a set of antlers. The Chimneys got their name because the one on the right actually has a hollow area at the top, similar to a chimney. The many dead trees visible from here are Eastern hemlocks killed by a non-native insect, the hemlock woolly adelgid.

About two miles later, the road makes a 360-degree loop, spiraling over itself as it climbs higher. Officially, such a formation is called a helix, but informally, this one is called **The Loop**. (Have the kids watch for the yellow diamond-shaped road sign announcing it.)

About 1.5 miles further on is the trailhead for the **Alum Cave Trail** (4.6 miles roundtrip, to Alum Cave and back; or 11 miles roundtrip to the summit of Mount Le Conte and back; see the chapter on hikes with a view).

About four miles further is **Morton Overlook** (named for a Knoxville mayor from the 1920s), a wowzer of a vista. You can see the Chimney Tops again from here (although you'll be looking down on them this time), along with **Mt. Mingus** (the highest peak on the left). This is one of the most photographed views in the Smokies.

In less than a mile, you'll be at Newfound Gap.

Newfound Gap: In addition to the state line between Tennessee and North Carolina, you'll find a few additional things to discover here. Most notable is the vast view from the overlook. Even jaded locals rarely tire of this vista.

You'll also find stone steps to a rather grand platform known as the **Rockefeller Memorial**, in honor of the $5 million donation John D. Rockefeller, Jr., made in his mother's name when the land for the park was being acquired. It took stonemasons almost a year to build this platform, which is where Franklin D. Roosevelt stood when he dedicated the park in 1940.

The famous **Appalachian Trail**, a 2,175-mile

hiking trail that goes from Georgia to Maine, also crosses over New-found Gap Road (U.S. 441) at this spot (see the chapter on other family-fun hikes). Last but not least, you'll also find restrooms not far from the memorial.

Clingmans Dome: 0.1 mile south of Newfound Gap, you can take a popular side road, the seven-mile Clingmans Dome Road (closed in winter), which takes about 20 minutes one-way. At the end of the road is the trailhead for the paved walk to Clingmans Dome (one mile roundtrip; see the chapter on hikes with a view), the highest peak in the Smokies and third highest in the eastern U.S. You'll also find the trailhead for the Forney Ridge Trail, which is the way to Andrews Bald (3.6 miles roundtrip; see the chapter on hikes with a view). Finally, you'll see an information center and bookstore built by the Civilian Conervation Corps (CCC) at the start of the trail to Clingmans Dome. Restrooms are located in the parking area.

From North Carolina toward Newfound Gap: About a half mile after the Oconaluftee Visitor Center, you'll see **Mingus Mill** (closed in winter; see the chapter on self-guiding nature trails), a working gristmill dating from 1886. You'll find restrooms beside the parking lot.

Smokemont Campground (see the chapter on camping) is just under three miles further, and less than two miles after that is the **Collins Creek Picnic Area** (closed in winter; see the chapter on picnicking).

The most impressive overlook on this side is eight miles further at the **Webb Overlook** (on the left), named for Asheville, NC, newspaper publisher Charles A. Webb. This is one of the best views of Clingmans Dome in the park. You can also see the Deep Creek valley, toward Bryson City, from here.

After driving three more miles, you'll be at Newfound Gap.

Cades Cove Loop Road

Cades Cove is where Mother Nature and Father Time meet. This **11-mile, one-way loop road** winds through forest and wide-open fields alike, making it the **best place in the park for wildlife viewing**. It also boasts log homes, barns, churches, a gristmill, and other historic structures dating from the 1800s. In fact, you'll find more historic buildings here than in any other area of the park, and you're free to explore them all.

The loop generally takes from two to four hours to tour, depending on how many times you want to get out of the car and how many

FUN factivity

Your kids will have fun with this bottle experiment that shows the effect of air pressure at different altitudes. Take a half full water or soft drink bottle with a screw top cap with you when you drive to Newfound Gap. When you get up there, you'll notice that the bottle feels rather firm and rigid. That's because air pressure decreases as you climb in altitude, so the pressure inside the bottle is greater than the pressure outside. Take the cap off, and then screw it back on again. Now the pressure is the same, both inside and out. Feel the difference? Then, leaving the cap on, watch what happens after you drive back down the mountain. By the time you get to the bottom, the bottle will definitely look squooshed! At the lower elevations, air pressure is greater outside the bottle than inside.

The view from Clingmans Dome tower.

"bear jams" you encounter. Please be considerate of your fellow travelers, and use the pull-offs if you want to stop to view wildlife—don't stop in the road, blocking traffic.

Note that the loop road is closed from sunset to sunrise. From early May through late September, it's also closed to motor vehicles on Wednesday and Saturday mornings until 10 a.m. so that bicyclists and walkers can enjoy the cove (see the chapter on biking). You can rent bikes (with helmets) from the Cades Cove Campground store just before the start of the loop road.

More than two million people each year drive the loop road through Cades Cove.

Another option is to take one of the new **Cades Cove Heritage Tours**, sponsored by a private, nonprofit organization that partners with the Great Smoky Mountains Heritage Center in Townsend (see the chapter on sites outside the park). The best part of these tours (which last three to four hours, longer in busy seasons) is the guide who tells stories about the cove and its former residents along the way.

The fuel-efficient busses hold 19 passengers, and trips leave from the depot next to the Heritage Center every day at 8 a.m. and 1 p.m., but contact the company for exact schedules (1-865-448-8838 or www.cadescoveheritagetours.org). Discounts are available for kids (and those under age six are free), seniors, and members of the Heritage Center. You can also get discounts if you buy a combo ticket for both the tour and the Heritage Center.

Here's a brief description of what you'll find where along the loop, but keep your eyes peeled at all times for wildlife, more plentiful near

The first white settlers arrived in Cades Cove in 1818, and by 1850, more than 700 people lived here. The pioneers were farmers—raising corn, wheat, oats, rye, sorghum and vegetables —and tending to pigs, sheep, and cattle. But they also hunted wild game and made good use of the wild chestnuts, berries, greens, and herbs they found growing in the surrounding area.

dawn and dusk. You might encourage your kids to keep a count of how many of each type of animal they see. Chances are they'll lose count of the white-tailed deer. Other favorite sightings here include black bear, red fox, wild turkey, raccoon, and even an occasional coyote dashing across the road.

If you want to shorten your loop, you can take either of two shortcuts (**Sparks Lane or Hyatt Lane**) to the other side of the loop. Be aware that unlike on the loop road itself, traffic is two-way on each of these side roads.

The only year-round rest room facilities here are at the **Cades Cove Picnic Area** and the **Cades Cove Campground** before the entrance to the loop road, and at the **Cades Cove Visitor Center**, at about the halfway point. You'll also find a small camp store and snack bar at the campground (open from mid-March through early November.

At the orientation shelter at the entrance to the loop road, rangers are on hand during the summer to answer questions, supply park maps, and sell various books on the cove.

The first stop you encounter is also one of the most

John and Lucretia Oliver built this cabin (left) in the early 1820s. Pictured above is their descendent John W. Oliver and his wife Nancy Whitehead Oliver.

notable. The **John Oliver Place** (a quarter-mile walk from the parking area) is the oldest log home in Cades Cove, dating from the early 1820s. Oliver and his wife, Lucretia, who had 10 children, were the first white settlers in the cove. In all, five generations of Olivers lived here for more than a hundred years before they were forced to make way for park establishment.

Several small churches come next. The **Primitive Baptist Church** dates from 1887, the **Methodist Church** was built in 1902, and the **Missionary Baptist Church** dates from 1915. Feel free to explore the graveyards, too, although take care not to walk on the graves themselves. You'll see graves with birth dates as early as the 1700s as well as graves from modern times—those who can prove they are descended from a family with Smokies roots can be buried here.

At the Primitive Baptist Church (down a turn-off that takes you a quarter mile from the loop road), ask your kids to find the grave of William Hamby, who was in the North Carolina militia during the Revolutionary War.

If you visit in March or April, look for bunches of daffodils. That's a sure sign that a house once stood nearby, since the cove residents often planted them in their gardens. Across from the Missionary Baptist Church, see if your kids can identify the letters and numbers that are spelled out by the daffodils planted between the church and Tater Branch (a stream). A company of the Civilian Conservation Corps planted bulbs so that the blooms would show the name of their camp.

The **Elijah Oliver Place** is next, down a half-mile gravel trail from the main loop road. The son of John Oliver, whose home was the first stop on the drive, built this house, part of which dates from 1930. This is one of the most intact 19th-century farmsteads in the park.

Be sure to explore the various outbuildings here. The springhouse was not just a water source. It also did double duty as a refrigerator, keeping foods like milk, eggs, and butter cold. The smokehouse was for preserving and storing meat. The corncrib held corn until it could be ground into cornmeal. The barn sheltered both farm equipment and animals (milk cows and the horses, oxen, and mules used to pull plows).

Coming up next, the gravel road on the right leads to the trailhead for the **Abrams Falls Trail** (five miles roundtrip; see the chapter on waterfall hikes).

Next stop is the **Cades Cove Visitor Center**, with its adjacent historic **Cable Mill** area (see the chapter on visitor centers). As you leave the visitor center parking lot, if you wish to visit the **Henry Whitehead Place**, make a sharp right-hand turn onto the dirt road (Forge Creek Road) leading away from the loop road.

Early pioneer families in Cades Cove often had 10 or 12 children! School was only in session during the winter months when the kids weren't needed to help in the fields.

The **Dan Lawson Place** is next, dating from 1856. Look at the brick chimney, built with handmade bricks. At the **Tipton Place**, dating from 1870, you'll find a number of outbuildings,

The Noah "Bud" Ogle cabin.

including a blacksmith shop, a carpentry shop, a bee gum shelter (once housing honeybees), and a cantilevered barn, among others.

The last building is the relatively tiny (and quite cute) **Carter Shields Cabin**, once owned by a veteran of the Civil War Battle of Shiloh.

Roaring Fork Motor Nature Trail
Closed in winter

This outstandingly pretty drive through deep woods follows a rushing mountain stream that the route crosses several times. The wooded and windy drive is often less crowded than Cades Cove and has historic structures of its own you can visit. Note that it's closed from sunset to sunrise.

To get there, turn off the main parkway in Gatlinburg at traffic light #8 and follow Historic Nature Trail/Airport Road to the Cherokee Orchard Road entrance to the national park. This route (from light #8 to where loop drive ends at Low Gap Road outside of Gatlinburg) is nine miles and takes about an hour to drive, not counting stops.

You'll first come to the **Noah "Bud" Ogle Self-Guiding Nature Trail** (0.75 mile roundtrip; see the chapter on self-guiding nature trails), a walk through what was once the Ogle farm. The next road marker is #2, the trailhead for the **Rainbow Falls, Bullhead, and Old Sugarlands trails**. By far the most popular footpath here is the trail to Rainbow Falls (5.4 miles roundtrip; see the chapter on waterfall hikes). Restrooms (vault toilets) are available near the trailhead.

Just beyond the trailheads is the start of the 5.5-mile, one-way **Roaring Fork Motor Nature Trail** (closed in winter). At marker #5 is the trailhead for the **Trillium Gap Trail**, which is the way to **Grotto Falls** (2.4 miles roundtrip; see the chapter on waterfall hikes), where you can actually walk behind the waterfall. Restrooms (vault toilets) are available at this trailhead. To hike to Grotto Falls in winter, you can walk to the trailhead from the Rainbow Falls trailhead, which adds 2.3 miles each way.

Marker #10 denotes the **Jim Bales place**, while #11 marks the **Ephraim Bales home**. Ephraim and his wife Minerva had nine children and farmed 30 of their 70 acres. Ask your kids to find the Granny hole, a tiny square window in their double log cabin.

At marker #12 is the fancier (and more colorful) **Alfred Reagan Place**. Reagan was a jack-of-all-trades, spending time as a carpenter, blacksmith, shopkeeper, miller, and even a lay preacher. Check out his tub mill across the road from his house. It's so close to the road it could almost be a drive-up cornmeal shop.

FUN fact

As you're driving on Cherokee Orchard Road on your way to the Roaring Fork Motor Nature Trail, you will pass the Twin Creeks Science and Education Center, tucked back in the woods. This building (which is not open to the public) is the brand new headquarters for the park's resource management staff— the folks who study the park's air and water quality, among other things. The building also houses office and lab space for the many visiting scientists who come to the Smokies each year to study the amazing number of plants and animals. Twin Creeks also provides state-of-the-art facilities for the park's 50,000-specimen natural history collection.

The Place of a Thousand Drips.

Marker #15 indicates a spot on the left called **The Place of a Thousand Drips**, a tall, rocky cliff that has either barely a trickle of water during dry spells or a series of cascading waterfalls in rainy weather.

The end of the Motor Nature Trail deposits you outside the park. Turn left to return to downtown Gatlinburg and the entrance to the park. You will eventually come to a traffic light on Highway 321. Left takes you to downtown, right goes out 321 to Greenbrier, Cosby, and eventually Interstate 40.

A few miles after turning onto Heintooga Ridge Road is the Masonic Monument at Black Camp Gap. The fraternal order of the Masons built this curious-looking obelisk in 1938. The 12-foot-tall structure, nine feet square at its base, is made of 687 stones from most states in the U.S., plus 41 countries. Stones from all seven continents have been cemented into the structure, which also boasts stones from the Alamo, the Rock of Gibraltar, the White House, and Plymouth Rock.

Cataloochee Auto Tour

Think of Cataloochee as the next chapter in history after Cades Cove. Whereas the Tennessee community is filled mostly with log cabins, Cataloochee is the **best place in the park to see historic frame buildings** (those built with boards instead of logs) from the late 19th and early 20th centuries.

The first home in Cataloochee Valley went up in 1814, and a hundred years later, more than 1,200 people lived here, the biggest settlement in the Smokies. They built more than 200 buildings, although today only a handful still stand—two churches, a school, and several homes and outbuildings. The people who settled here were mainly farmers, and many also planted and tended apple orchards. Some families also got into the tourism business early, providing room and board for fisherman and other tourists.

Restroom facilities at Cataloochee are limited to vault toilets at the Palmer Place and at the campground (which is open only from early March through October; see the chapter on camping). You are welcome to use the restrooms at the campground even if you aren't camping, by the way.

It's a bit ironic that Cataloochee was so busy in its heyday, because it's relatively remote today. To get there from I-40, take exit #20 in North Carolina. After 0.2 mile, turn right onto Cove Creek Road and follow the signs 11 miles into the Cataloochee Valley. To get there from the Oconaluftee Visitor Center or Cherokee, take the Blue Ridge Parkway to Highway 19. Follow this road through Maggie Valley and turn left onto Highway 276 N. Just before the entrance ramp to I-40, turn left and follow the signs 11 miles to Cataloochee.

FUN *factivity*

Have your kids look at the old post office sign in one of the exhibits at the Palmer Place. See if they can find anything funny (e.g., backwards) about it.

With either route, the last three of these 11 miles are down a narrow, but well-maintained, gravel road. When you see the paved road, turn left onto it. Take the next gravel drive on the right just a little bit to the **Palmer Place**, where you'll also find restrooms. (If you pass the campground, you've gone too far.) This is where the auto tour begins.

If you have time and you're up for adventure, you can also get to Cataloochee via a bumpy 16-mile gravel road (once called the Old Cataloochee Turnpike and now called Old North Carolina 284) that starts on the state line one mile before Big Creek (10 miles east of Cosby). This windy, slow-going route is generally fine for cars (although not RVs) and definitely provides a backwoods driving experience. Have the kids keep a lookout for wildlife along the way. Near the end of the drive, when the road comes to a T-intersection, turn right. You'll be at the Palmer Place in less than two miles.

Here's what to expect from the Cataloochee Valley drive, which is 2.5 miles one-way. (Try to time your visit so you're done near dusk, because that's the time when you can typically see the most elk in the fields by the road.)

The Palmer House was originally a double log cabin built in 1860, although siding was added about 1902. The two rooms in the back (including a kitchen) were added about 1924. In those back rooms you'll find some historic exhibits and old photos.

Drive toward the paved road and turn right, continuing past the **Cataloochee Campground** (closed in winter). In the wide field you'll pass the **Will Messer Barn**, set back from the road. Dating from around 1900, the barn was moved here from a nearby area. (The house near it is a private residence; the Cataloochee Ranger Station is around the back of the building.)

Next comes the **Palmer Chapel**, a Methodist Church built in 1903 and remodeled in 1929. Most preachers in these parts were called circuit riders—they didn't preach in only one place but traveled around in a circuit, visiting once a month.

Across the bridge, the road becomes gravel. Park here and take the very short walk to the **Beech Grove School**, nestled back in the woods. This white clapboard school building, dating from 1903, has two rooms and very tall windows. Sitting at the desks, you can still hear the stream rushing outside.

The **Caldwell House**, built in 1903, is next on the drive. It's a two-story white clapboard home with sky blue trim. This is a more modern home complete with closets and fairly fancy paneling. Have your kids read the peeling catalogue copy that's pasted on the walls upstairs. It advertises clothing and various other necessities (like boys rubber hi-cut boots). You can even find an ad offering to cure stammering!

At the end of the road, you can park and walk down the **Rough Fork Trail** to the Woody House (two miles roundtrip). Rough is right, as roads go. Once a dirt road, this delightful trail winding through the forest and crossing back and forth over the water at times resembles a dry streambed more than a road!

The **Woody House** is a two-story, white clapboard home with a shingle-shake roof. It started out as a one-room log cabin that was enlarged and improved in 1900. Lichens hang on the trees outside, and the ornate woodwork makes a pretty design. A set of well-worn steps leads upstairs to three rooms.

Balsam Mountain Loop
Closed in winter

FUN fact

Heintooga comes from the Cherokee word Iyentooga, which means hiding place or refuge, or literally, a dwelling in the wilderness. The terrain you see from the overlook at the Heintooga Picnic Area includes the mountains where many Cherokee hid when the government was rounding them up in the 1830s for the tragic forced trek to Oklahoma now known as the Trail of Tears.

This 47-mile loop drive actually involves a number of roads, both in and out of the national park, at some rather high elevations with stunning views. It's also one of the **best drives for summer wildflowers.** Part of the road is gravel, but it's fairly easy to navigate in a car (although RVs should not attempt it). The whole loop takes a little more than two hours, not counting stops.

Start at the Oconaluftee Visitor Center and go toward Cherokee for one mile, turning onto the Blue Ridge Parkway near the park boundary. The great views and many pull-offs begin right away—on both sides of the road. Some of the best include the **Thomas Divide Overlook** (after five miles) and the **Big Witch Overlook** (after seven miles).

After about 11 miles on the Blue Ridge Parkway, which will take about 20 minutes, turn off at milepost 458, where you see the big sign for Balsam Mountain. This is actually Heintooga Ridge Road. In a few miles, you'll cross back into Great Smoky Mountains National Park on this windy, scenic route that offers spectacular views on both the right and left.

Eight miles after making the turn, you'll pass the **Balsam Mountain Campground** (closed in winter). At about a mile high, this is the highest-elevation campground in the park. Inside the campground is the trailhead for the **Balsam Mountain Self-Guiding Nature Trail**

Mingo Falls.

(1.5 miles roundtrip; see the chapter on self-guiding nature trails), with its gazillion blackberry bushes that provide a sweet treat in summer.

Just half a mile farther, the paved road ends at the **Heintooga Picnic Area** (closed in winter; see the chapter on picnicking). You'll find restrooms near the parking area, and an absolutely spectacular overlook behind the picnic area at the start of the **Flat Creek Trail** (5.2 miles roundtrip; see the chapter on other family-fun hikes). This part of the drive, from where you left the Blue Ridge Parkway to the picnic area, will take about 30 minutes.

You could turn around and return the way you came, but to continue the loop drive, turn onto the one-way, gravel Balsam Mountain Road (although the sign reads, "Heintooga-Round Bottom Road"), which follows a narrow-gauge railroad bed from logging days. The 17-mile drive from here to the park boundary at the Cherokee reservation takes about an hour. (The last four of its 17 miles are two-way, and the name here changes to Straight Fork Road.)

Where the paved road begins again, you are now outside the park and on the **Cherokee reservation**. A short distance later, the road

Interior of the Walker sisters' cabin circa 1940. Magazines wallpapered the walls.

At right: Four of the seven Walker sisters living in the cabin in 1946.

dead-ends at Big Cove Road. Turn left here, toward downtown Cherokee, which is a 10-mile drive. Not quite halfway back to Cherokee, you can stop at **Mingo Falls**. To find the falls, cross the small bridge on the left at the sign for Mingo Falls Campground. These pretty falls are 120 feet high, among the highest in the southern Appalachians, and the trail to get there and back is a half mile roundtrip.

Continue on Big Cove Road until it ends at U.S. 441. A left turn will take you into downtown Cherokee, and if you turn right you'll return to the park entrance and the Oconaluftee Visitor Center.

Little River Road

Little River Road is one of the prettiest drives in the park because the meandering Little River (ironically one of the larger rivers in the park) with its big gray boulders, mini-cascades, and sun-dappled surface follows the road most of the way. It's an 18-mile stretch from its start at the Sugarlands Visitor Center to its end at the park's Townsend entrance, but the twists and turns make the drive about 45 minutes. Along this road you'll encounter the trailhead to **Laurel Falls** (2.5 miles roundtrip; see the chapter on waterfall hikes) and a turnoff leading to both the **Elkmont Campground** and the **Elkmont Self-guiding Nature Trail** (0.75 mile roundtrip).

Little River Road also takes you to the **Metcalf Bottoms Picnic Area**, where the trailhead is located for the Metcalf Bottoms Trail leading to the **Little Greenbrier School** (1.2 miles roundtrip). (You can also take a one-mile drive from the picnic area on the Little Greenbrier Road across the bridge to get to the school, although the road is closed in winter.) At the schoolhouse, you can extend your hike along the Little Brier Gap Trail to the **Walker sisters' cabin** (an additional 2.2 miles roundtrip). (See the chapter on other family-fun hikes for descriptions of both of these options.)

From here on, the road has more bends in it than a slinky. You can round a turn and suddenly face a waterfall that's gone in a few seconds as the road twists in a new direction. In fact, the 28-foot **Meigs Falls** can be seen tucked back about 300 feet from the road at marker #6. Drive with care and use the pull-offs.

Little River Road technically ends at the **Townsend "Y"** (the intersection of the road to Townsend), although the roadway continues as Laurel Creek Road, leading seven miles to Cades Cove.

Foothills Parkway

The Foothills Parkway is situated outside the main body of the park, but it falls under national park jurisdiction. This road is in two parts— an 18-mile segment at the western end of the park near Townsend and a 6-mile stretch on the northeastern corner by Cosby. (Both sections, by the way, are very good places to watch sunrise or sunset.)

Foothills Parkway West starts from Route 321, nine miles west of Townsend. Following a ridgeline, it offers overlooks with stunning views on both sides of the road, making it one of the most scenic drives in the Smokies (with just a fraction of the traffic, even in high season).

The **Look Rock** area, roughly at the segment's midpoint, is the highlight. From here, you can also take the trail to the Look Rock tower (one mile roundtrip; see the chapter on hikes with a view) for a 360-degree vista that is every bit as fine as the view from Clingmans Dome (but less crowded).

The parkway ends at U.S. 129, near Chilhowee, and the drive is about 30 minutes, not counting stops.

Foothills Parkway East connects I-40 at exit #443 to Tennessee 32 at Cosby. Its best views of the Smokies are the two overlooks closest to the Cosby end on the south side of the road. The total drive time for this portion of the parkway is 15 minutes.

FUN factivity

Have your kids look at the rock cliffs along Little River Road to see if they can identify Indian Head Rock, which resembles a man's profile. (The spot is 15 miles from where the road begins at the Sugarlands Visitor Center, or three miles from its other end at the Townsend "Y.") The road curves around this large rock, an outcropping that rises 50 feet and juts way out above the roadway. In 2006, a big chunk of the rock under the "chin" fell into the road. Special engineers trained to work with rock faces glued and bolted it back into place, ensuring the landmark will remain for generations to come.

CHAPTER 7

Ranger Programs and Educational Opportunities

Whether your kids spend an hour discussing animal poop with a ranger or join a 10-day family adventure hiking, swimming, sightseeing, and stargazing with you in the heart of the park, you're bound to give the Smokies an A for the park's amazingly fun and creative learning opportunities. Here are some of the options:

Ranger programs

The Smokies have an unusually large number of free, fun, and fabulous ranger programs during the spring, summer, and fall. Exact offerings tend to change from year to year and even from season to season, but they all have one thing in common: getting kids excited about the plants, animals, and cultural history of the park through hands-on activities.

For example, your kids might join a ranger to hike through the woods to view waterfalls, splash through streams in search of salamanders, create an old-fashioned mountain toy, weave a bookmark on a loom using techniques from the early settlers, learn to play the dulcimer (a.k.a. hog fiddle), make a clay pot the way the Cherokee did, fashion a dinner bell in a 19th-century blacksmith shop, or act out characters from old-fashioned Smoky Mountain stories. One popular program teaches kids how to use GPS (global positioning system) technology. Rangers also hold evening campfire programs, host sunset talks at Clingmans Dome, and take kids on night hikes.

Most ranger programs last anywhere from 30 minutes to one and a half hours, and the meeting points include all three visitor centers, several campgrounds, as well as many other areas throughout the park. For a schedule of offerings, pick up a copy of the free *Smokies Guide* park newspaper at any visitor center or check the park's website at www.nps.gov/grsm/planyourvisit/events.htm.

Only one ranger program has a fee—the morning and evening hayrides around Cades Cove from the Cades Cove Riding Stables (closed in winter; see the chapter on horseback riding).

FUN fact

The pioneers joked that the Smokies were so steep that the only way to sow their seeds was to stand on one slope, load a shotgun with seeds, and shoot the seeds over to the next hill.

Junior Rangers
(and Not-So-Junior Rangers)

If your kids want to be park rangers, here's their chance. The Smokies has an award-winning Junior Ranger Program, designed for children ages five through 12. Here's how it works. First, stop at one of the park's visitor centers to buy your child a Junior Ranger booklet, available for a few dollars. Get the booklet that's appropriate for the child's age. There are four: one for ages five and six, one for ages seven and eight, another for ages nine and 10, and a fourth for ages 11 and 12.

Once the child completes the required activities in the booklet (including things like going on a leaf scavenger hunt or doing a crossword puzzle themed to a historic area), picks up one grocery-sack size bag of litter, and attends any ranger program, then you can stop off at any visitor center to see a park ranger. The ranger will give your child a certificate and a Junior Ranger pin.

During summer, another option may be to pick up a free Junior Ranger program card at any visitor center for each of your kids. The same card is good for any age child. Once your child attends any three Junior Ranger programs and collects the rangers' signatures to prove it, he or she can also receive a Junior Ranger certificate and pin.

Adults don't need to feel left out any more. Anyone over the age of 13 who wants to get in on the fun can now join the new Not-So-Junior Ranger program. Just pick up a free program card (shaped like a ranger's head!) from any visitor center, attend three ranger programs and get the rangers' signatures, and then return to any visitor center to receive a certificate and a special patch.

The Great Smoky Mountains
Institute at Tremont

This nonprofit environmental education center located in the watershed of the Middle Prong of the Little River turns the park into a combination playground and outdoor classroom. The institute offers three- to 10-day overnight programs year-round that highlight the cultural and natural history of the Smokies for kids, families, teachers, and seniors.

Kids' summer camps include both five- and 10-night programs for teens and pre-teens, including:
• *Discovery Camp* (ages 9-12)

FUN *fact*

About 115 archaeological sites have been found so far in the national park, including prehistoric Native American sites as well as historic sites from the pioneer days. Volunteers sometimes help park staff conduct archaeological surveys and excavations.

- *Wilderness Adventure Trek* (ages 13-17)
- *Backcountry Ecology Expedition Camp* (ages 13-17)
- *Teen High Adventure Camp* (ages 13-17)
- *Field Ecology Adventure Camp* (ages 13-17)

New programs are added occasionally, such as the new science camp just for girls entering eighth grade.

Family offerings include the two-night **Family Adventure Weekend** (in winter) and the five-night **Smoky Mountains Family Camp** (in summer). These programs include activities such as hikes, crafts, games, wildlife demonstrations, sightseeing, swimming, campfires, and downtime just to hang with your family in the park.

Participants either stay in the climate-controlled dorms with modern bathrooms or they camp out (using tents from the institute). Hearty meals are served family style in the dining hall.

A few day programs also exist, such as citizen science programs that allow kids and adults alike to assist with real scientific research, like monarch butterfly tagging in the fall and salamander monitoring in summer.

Tremont also has a bookstore/gift shop (and a vending machine with cold drinks).

For program dates and costs, call the Great Smoky Mountains Institute at Tremont at 1-865-448-6709 or visit the institute's website at www.gsmit.org.

FUN fact

When the Great Smoky Mountains Institute at Tremont was founded in 1969, it was one of the first environmental education centers in the U.S. to be located inside a national park.

The Smoky Mountain Field School

The Smoky Mountain Field School offers one-, two-, and five-day field courses from March through November covering such topics as environmental studies, backcountry hiking, foraging, wildlife, wildflowers, botanical photography, and crafts. Begun in 1978, the Field School is part of the continuing education division of the University of Tennessee-Knoxville and is run jointly with the National Park Service. The instructors are experts in their fields, and many of them are UT professors.

Families with kids aged six to 12 can sign up for summer family programs that involve, among other activities, catching pollywogs, salamanders, and insects; hiking to waterfalls; and searching for animal tracks. These are day programs—no lodging is included. Adults must accompany their kids (no more than two children per adult).

For program dates and costs, call the Smoky Mountain Field School at 1-865-974-0150 or visit the field school's website at www.outreach.utk.edu/smoky.

The Smokies is also home to the Appalachian Highlands Science Learning Center, located at 5,000 feet on Purchase Knob on the park's eastern edge. This is part of a network created by Congress of 17 such centers to support research and education about science in our national parks. (A total of 32 will exist eventually.) Student-scientist programs are available for school groups here, although no programs are offered to the general public.

SMOKY MOUNTAIN ROADSIDE BINGO

Look for the various objects in the squares below. When you find one, mark the square with an "X." When you get a whole row of X's, (vertically, horizontally, or diagonally), you win!

Picnic Area	Waterfall	Park Ranger	Deer	Gravestone
Trailhead Sign	Ranger Station	Hemlock Tree	Quiet Walkway	Log Cabin
Mt. Le Conte	Wild Turkey	FREE	Tunnel	Sycamore Tree
Nature Trail	Numbered Post	NPS Arrowhead Sign	Butterfly	Visitor Center
Squirrel	Cantileavered Barn	Split Rail Fence	Wildflower	Log Bridge

Trailhead Sign: LUMBER RIDGE TRAIL

NPS Arrowhead Sign: GREAT SMOKY MOUNTAINS NATIONAL PARK

CHAPTER 8

Picnicking

If you spend much time at all in the Smokies, chances are you'll be picnicking sooner rather than later. In truth, there are as many great picnic spots in this park as there are hairs on a black bear's hide. They'll appear almost instantly whenever young stomachs start to growl—large, flat rocks by streambeds, mossy logs by the edge of trails, or boulders near the foot of waterfalls.

For families in search of something a smidgen less *au naturel*, the park maintains 10 formally designated picnic areas, each offering tables (most of them on leveled gravel areas), grills, and restrooms. Several picnic areas also include pavilions that can be reserved for large groups. (Additionally, you can reserve picnic pavilions at Twin Creeks and Greenbrier that are not adjacent to a picnic area.) Most of the picnic areas are open year-round on a first-come, first-served basis. Three (Heintooga, Look Rock, and Collins Creek) are closed in winter. Several are handicapped accessible.

Be sure to throw your food scraps and other trash in the bear-proof trash receptacles at each area, and clean your grill before you leave. If you leave any food on the tables, fire pits, grills, or on the ground, it will attract bears. As the park saying goes, a fed bear is a dead bear.

Here are descriptions of each official picnic area, as well as one unofficial but incredibly popular picnic spot. Where you see references to campgrounds, self-guiding nature trails, and stables, see the appropriate chapters in this book for more detail.

Metcalf Bottoms

Metcalf Bottoms along Little River Road is one of the larger and more popular picnic areas, with 165 sites (including two that are handicapped accessible). Tables line the banks of the Little River in either direction as you drive in, and a few are tucked back into the woods. There's even a spot here (on the left side) to play horseshoes. A covered pavilion can be reserved for large groups either online (at www.recreation.gov) or by calling 1-877-444-6777. The fee is around $20.

From the picnic area, you can drive over the bridge and then take the first right down the gravel road (closed in winter) for one mile to get to the historic **Little Greenbrier School**. Or you could hike there

The Chimneys Picnic Area.

via the Metcalf Bottoms Trail (1.2 miles roundtrip). Once you're at the school, you can extend your hike along the Little Brier Gap Trail to the **Walker sisters' cabin** (an additional 2.2 miles roundtrip; see the chapter on other family-fun hikes for descriptions of both trails).

Cades Cove

Water flows on either side of the **Cades Cove Picnic Area**, so many of the 81 sites (three of which are handicapped accessible) are streamside. To get to the Cades Cove Picnic Area, turn left off of Laurel Creek Road just as you approach the start of the Cades Cove Loop Road (see the chapter on scenic drives). The turnoff immediately forks, and the picnic area is to the left. (Cades Cove Riding Stables is to the right.)

The camp store at the campground (open from mid-March through early November) sells various picnic supplies, in case you forgot any or need something additional. If you forgot food altogether, you can even get lunch at the camp store's snack bar. This picnic area closes at 8 p.m. in the summer and at sunset during the rest of the year.

Collins Creek
Closed in winter

With 182 sites (two of which are handicapped accessible), Collins Creek is the largest picnic area in the park. This spacious picnic area (closed in winter) is on Newfound Gap Road (U.S. 441), within two miles of the Smokemont Campground in North Carolina.

As you drive in, you have two choices. If you go straight ahead and up the hill, you'll be at the larger of the two areas. If you instead turn left and go down the hill, you'll find a smaller bunch of picnic sites along a creek. A covered pavilion can be reserved for large groups either online (at www.recreation.gov) or by calling 1-877-444-6777. The fee is around $20. This picnic area closes at 8 p.m. in the summer and at sunset during the rest of the year.

Chimneys

Just five miles from the Sugarlands Visitor Center on Newfound Gap Road (U.S. 441), the 89-site **Chimneys Picnic Area** is a very popular spot. To get to a site by the rocky, slow-moving stream (perhaps near a small cascade), drive to the far end of the picnic area and follow the road as it loops back down toward the entrance again.

The Chimneys Picnic Area is also where you'll find the trailhead for the **Cove Hardwood Self-Guiding Nature Trail** (0.75 mile roundtrip), widely considered the park's best spring wildflower walk, but an excellent trail any time of the year. This picnic area closes at 8 p.m. in the summer and at sunset during the rest of the year.

The Chimneys Picnic Area used to be a park ampground (one of the first two in the park), which closed in 1969.

Cosby

The **Cosby Picnic Area** off of Route 32 along the northern boundary of the park is located at the entrance to the National Park Service Cosby Campground (closed in winter). You can hear Cosby Creek as it flows through the area, although none of the 95 wooded picnic sites here is actually streamside. A covered pavilion can be reserved for large groups either online (at www.recreation.gov) or by calling 1-877-444-6777. The fee is around $20.

As you drive in, you'll pass the trailhead for the **Gabes Mountain Trail**, which you can hike partway to Hen Wallow Falls (4.4 miles roundtrip; see the chapter on waterfall hikes). You can also take the Cosby Nature Trail (one mile roundtrip), a simply magical walk beginning near the amphitheater in the campground. You'll also be a short drive from the Foothills Parkways East (see the chapter on scenic drives).

Greenbrier

Just 6 miles east of Gatlinburg on Route 321 is the Greenbrier entrance, leading to several trailheads, the tiny **Greenbrier Picnic Area**, and a separate picnic pavilion. You'll see only 12 official picnic sites in this relatively uncrowded section of the park. But you'll find countless accommodating rocks and pull-offs along the drive, which follows a lovely stretch of rollicking creek.

This is also where you'll find the trailhead for the **Porters Creek Trail** (two miles roundtrip; see the chapter on other family-fun hikes). This is a particularly lovely hike during

The Greenbrier area of the park once included four gristmills, two churches, two stores, two blacksmith shops, a school, and three cemeteries, not to mention the Greenbrier Hotel (also known as the Le Conte Hotel). After the park was established, a campground opened where the Greenbrier Picnic Area is today, operating from the early 1940s until 1973.

spring wildflower season. Drive to the one-way loop at the far end of Greenbrier Road to find the trailhead. (On the way, you'll pass a picnic pavilion on the right—a few miles from the regular picnic area described earlier—that can be reserved for large groups either online at www.recreation.gov or by calling 1-877-444-6777; the fee is around $10.)

If you drive here from the Sugarlands area, you'll pass the **Smoky Mountain Riding Stables** (closed in winter; see the chapter on horseback riding) on the way, just a few miles before the Greenbrier entrance.

Deep Creek

The **Deep Creek Picnic Area** is in a gorgeous section of the park near Bryson City, NC. After you drive into the park from the Deep Creek entrance, the 58-site picnic area is straight ahead past the turnoff to the **Deep Creek Campground** (closed in winter). The picnic sites on the right side of the picnic area are along the wide but tame creek, a popular spot for wading. Consequently, the picnic area also offers men's and women's dressing stations for changing, the only such changing stations in the national park. A covered pavilion can be reserved for large groups either online (at www.recreation.gov) or by calling 1-877-444-6777. The fee is around $20.

Past the picnic area at the end of the road are several trailheads for trails that, when linked together, create what's known informally as the **Three Waterfalls Loop** (2.4 miles roundtrip, although you can take shorter options; see the chapter on waterfalls hikes). This hiking route will take you past Juney Whank Falls, Tom Branch Falls, and Indian Creek Falls.

Look Rock
Closed in winter

At about the midpoint of the Foothills Parkway West (see the chapter on scenic drives) is the aptly named **Look Rock Overlook**. Just before the overlook's parking area (coming from the Townsend end) is the turnoff for the **Look Rock Campground** and the 51-site **Look Rock Picnic Area** (both closed in winter). To find the picnic spot, after the turnoff from the parkway, take the left fork in the road (instead of going straight, which leads to the campground). This somewhat rocky spot is probably the most primitive and well worn of the park's picnic areas. (Instead of grills, by the way, the sites have fire rings with grates.)

While you're here, you can get a stunning 360-degree view of the mountains by hiking the trail to the **Look Rock Tower** (about two miles roundtrip from the picnic area, or one mile roundtrip if you drive to the parking lot at the overlook and access the trail from there; see the chapter on hikes with a view).

Heintooga
Closed in winter

The **Heintooga Picnic Area** is literally over the top. After all, it comes complete with a truly stunning overlook at about a mile in elevation (5,535 feet, to be exact). This lovely and remote spot with 41 sites is about 20 miles from the Oconaluftee Visitor Center. To get

For a stunning 360-degree view of the mountains, hike the trail to Look Rock Tower.

there from Oconaluftee, take the Blue Ridge Parkway to milepost 458 and turn left at the big sign for Balsam Mountain. You'll actually be turning onto Heintooga Ridge Road (closed in winter). The picnic area is at the end of this not-quite-nine-mile road, which runs along a mountain ridge and offers magnificent views of its own on either side.

The first picnic tables you see here are the usual wooden sort you see everywhere else. But if you walk up the hill through the forest to the older section of the picnic area, you'll find tables made from huge stone slabs with half-log benches. These unusual tables (unlike any others in the park) are made with native stone and were crafted by the Civilian Conservation Corps (CCC) during the Depression. (By the way, the building at the far edge of the picnic area is a boarded-up restroom no longer in use, so be sure your kids stay clear of it.) If you visit in late summer, look for the blueberries growing at the top of the hill here.

The overlook is just behind and a bit below the picnic area on an old roadbed that is also the trailhead for the **Flat Creek Trail** (5.2 miles roundtrip; see the chapter on other family-fun hikes). You'll find blackberry bushes full of fruit in the summer growing along here.

For a shorter hike from this area (and one absolutely loaded with berries in summer), drive a half mile back down Heintooga Ridge Road (the way you came) to the **Balsam Mountain Campground** (closed in winter). Just inside the campground is the trailhead for the **Balsam Mountain Self-Guiding Nature Trail** (1.5 miles roundtrip).

Although the paved Heintooga Ridge Road ends at the picnic area and overlook, you'll also see the entrance to the one-way, gravel Balsam Mountain Road (although the sign for it reads "Heintooga-Round Bottom Road"). If you take this road, it eventually will lead you back to Cherokee (see the chapter on scenic drives).

(By the way, although this picnic area doesn't have handicapped-accessible sites, the bathrooms are handicapped accessible.)

Big Creek

The **Big Creek Picnic Area** features a large stream (hence the name) but the site is actually quite small, with fewer than a dozen tables in the middle of **Big Creek Campground** (the park's smallest developed campground; closed in winter). It has an extra-long double table perfect for a large group, while the rest of the picnic sites stretch out along the riverbank, each one in its own magic spot overlooking the water. In the middle of the row of picnic sites is a pretty wooden footbridge that crosses the river.

Despite its tiny size, Big Creek has a particularly well-done handicapped accessible picnic site, complete with a paved walkway leading to a modified picnic table.

Big Creek is rather remote, just over the border on the North Carolina side of the park. To get there from the Tennessee side, drive east on Route 321 from Gatlinburg to Cosby. Then turn right onto Route 32 toward Big Creek. When you hit the state line 10 miles after Cosby, the paved road ends and you'll drive on a gravel road for a mile before you get to Big Creek.

To get there from the North Carolina side of the park, take I-40 west to exit 451 and follow the road for two miles (paved only for the first mile) past the Walters Power Generating Station to the park's Big Creek entrance.

Note that although the Big Creek Campground closes in winter, the picnic area does indeed stay open year-round. However, the rest room facilities are limited in winter to a pit toilet—the other restrooms close when the campground closes.

The Townsend "Y"

Although this is not an official park picnic site, plenty of visitors to the Smokies discover that the Townsend "Y" (sometimes spelled Townsend Wye) provides pure picnicking paradise. This spot, where two forks of the Little River join near the Townsend entrance to the park, has a little bit of everything. It offers grassy banks perfect for sunning, as well as shaded spots along a pebble-strewn riverbank down below the roadway. The river is clear, broad, and peaceful here, perfect for wading and minnow watching.

What the "Y" doesn't have are tables, grills, or drinking fountains.

A WORD ON THE HIKING TRAILS
IN THIS BOOK

Some 800 miles of hiking trails crisscross the Smokies, only a small selection of which are described here. This book highlights those that are generally considered the best for families, although every family certainly has different abilities and interests. For that reason, the hikes are divided into several chapters, each with a special focus (self-guiding nature trails and history walks, waterfalls, great views, and an "other" chapter with various miscellaneous gems).

• **For each hike, the roundtrip mileage and difficulty level are noted.** Sometimes different options are presented in the descriptions of the hikes, so if you're looking for something longer or shorter, you may find it. What you won't find are recommendations for specific ages, because one family's six-year-old could easily out-hike another family's 12-year-old. You know your family best, so use the general difficulty rating as a guide, and feel free to ask the rangers at the information desks in the visitor centers for more specific advice to determine which hikes are best for you and yours.

• **Also remember that when hiking with children, it's best to switch your focus from reaching the top or hiking the whole trail to having fun no matter what.** Be prepared for frequent stops to examine flowers, bugs, mossy logs, rocks, streams, and the like. And don't hesitate to turn around if your kids have had enough. That way, they'll want to go hiking again another day. If you push them past their limits of physical stamina or interest, you could turn them off the trail for good.

That said, here are some very general guidelines for distances:

• **Toddlers** can easily handle most of the shorter self-guiding nature trails in this guide.

• **Most four- to six-year-olds** can hike one or two miles roundtrip without difficulty if it's not too challenging (not too steep, not too cold, not too hot—you get the picture).

• **Kids ages seven and eight** can handle more trail, maybe three or four miles (or a steeper short trail).

• **Most nine- and 10-year-olds** can handle any of the trails in this book, while **11- and 12-year-olds** may well out-hike you (unless you are a hardcore, backcountry, Appalachian-Trail-type veteran, of course).

For a successful adventure, be sure to read the chapter on **what families need to know** (especially the section on hiking safety) before you set out. This will give you some suggestions for what to bring and will help ensure you have a safe, comfortable, and fun time.

CHAPTER 9

Self-Guiding Nature Trails and Historic Walking Tours

The Smokies is all about making fun discoveries that deepen your understanding and enrich your experience of the park. Some of these your family will undoubtedly make on their own, while others the Park Service is quite happy to assist you with. This latter category includes the fun tidbits of information you can pick up when you take any of the park's 16 self-guiding nature trails and historic walking tours. For most, the Park Service provides brochures that are available for a nominal cost at both the visitor centers and on the honor system from boxes at the various trailheads.

Three of these self-guiding trails are longer or more arduous hikes that are described in other chapters of this book. (Laurel Falls is included in the chapter on waterfall hikes, while you'll find both Alum Cave and Clingmans Dome in the chapter on hikes with a view.)

Ten are self-guiding nature trails (most of them short loop trails ranging from 0.4 mile to one mile long) that were developed by park naturalists. Your kids will have fun finding the numbered posts along the way that correspond to information in the guide booklet. Please note that although all of these trails are fairly easy, they tend to be a bit rooty and rocky in spots, so except for the one paved nature trail (Sugarlands Valley), they're definitely not stroller material. Some also are a bit hilly, but you'll see plenty of half-log benches sprinkled about if a brief rest is required.

Mountain folk prized their sourwood honey, which generally tastes sweeter than clover honey. Before you go on the Fighting Creek Self-Guiding Nature Trail, purchase a jar of sourwood honey from any visitor center gift shop. Bring it on the walk, along with a few pieces of bread, simple crackers, or even apple slices to drizzle it on. As you proceed down the trail, have your kids read the labels on the trees. When they come across a sourwood tree, stop and enjoy your snack, telling them that the summertime blossoms from a tree such as this one is where the bees that made this honey got their nectar. (Don't forget to bring wet wipes—you'll need them!)

The final three self-guiding offerings are historic walking tours that focus on a specific site. What follows are quick descriptions of each, as well as a note about the park's Quiet Walkways.

The John Ownby cabin on the Fighting Creek Nature Trail.

Fighting Creek
One mile roundtrip

This nature trail starts behind the Sugarlands Visitor Center and features a farm site long grown over and reclaimed by the forest. This was once a small community named Forks of the River, with 25 farms, a church, a school, a store, a post office, a gristmill (for grain), and a sawmill (for lumber). The trail starts in what was once a cornfield, and the guide booklet indicates the subtle clues that show this land was not always as it appears today.

The short wooden bridge over an area of low water at the start of the trail is an excellent place for spotting salamanders. Where the trail first forks, you'll go left to continue on the nature trail. The trail to the right goes to **Cataract Falls** (0.7 mile roundtrip; see the chapter on waterfall hikes).

Along the way, you'll come across the ruins of a stone chimney and a rehabilitated single-story, one-room log cabin once belonging to John Ownby.

The trailhead for the **Gatlinburg Trail** (two miles one-way; see the chapter on other family-fun hikes) begins near this point, as well.

Have your kids look for the black bear paw prints in the pavement of the Sugarlands Valley Self-guiding Nature Trail. They were made by a real bear that ambled across the freshly poured concrete when the trail was constructed, leaving a little accidental graffiti. (The spot is almost halfway around the loop trail, on the right at the base of an informational display about it, past marker #4.)

Sugarlands Valley
0.5 mile roundtrip

Just a half mile up Newfound Gap Road (U.S. 441) from the Sugarlands Visitor Center, this wide, paved, and level nature trail winds like a sidewalk through the forest. It's perfect for both strollers and wheelchairs. The delightful trail leads through what was once a community before the national park was created. You will pass a few stone chimneys (one from a permanent residence, and two from summer vacation cottages) as well as what remains of an old stone wall.

Cove Hardwood
0.75 mile roundtrip

Here's a nature trail that's absolutely stellar in spring (peaking about the second week of April), although the primeval forest it takes you through is worth seeing at any time of year. The trailhead starts at the Chimneys Picnic Area (see the chapter on picnicking) on Newfound Gap Road (U.S. 441), 4.6 miles south from Sugarlands Visitor Center. Note that parts of this trail are rather steep.

The guide booklet helps explain how so many different tree varieties came to grow in the Smokies, including trees you typically don't see this far south. Although the trees you pass at the start of the trail are second growth, further down the trail they are so tall (more than 100 feet) that you'd probably need binoculars to see the leaves well enough to identify them. Some trees in this section are more than 200 years old!

Although the focus of this trail is the trees, another highlight is the scratches made by a bear on a yellow buckeye tree at post #4.

FUN fact

The park's archaeological collection includes 23,000 historical objects (like baskets and mountaineers' farming implements) and 100,000 archaeological artifacts (like Native American pottery and arrowheads). In addition, if you stacked the park's collection of all the old pamphlets, journal pages, photographs, etc. produced about the Smokies over the years, it would stand 155 feet tall!

Elkmont
0.8 mile roundtrip

This self-guiding nature trail starts in the middle of the popular **Elkmont Campground** (closed in winter; see the chapter on camping). To get there, take the turnoff for the campground from Little River Road, and then take the far left turn just before the check-in office for the campground. The trailhead is a short distance from here.

The Little River Lumber Company once heavily logged this land, and although new trees have grown to replace the virgin stands the loggers decimated, much evidence remains to tell the tale. The guide booklet teaches kids to be brilliant bio-detectives, reading the vegetative clues along the way. The last stop on the trail points out some stone steps and flagstones, challenging the reader to figure out what they're from. By this point, the answer should be elementary, my dear Watson.

Cades Cove
0.5 to one mile roundtrip

This half-mile nature trail in section C of the Cades Cove Campground (see the chapter on camping) has been around for a while, but it's recently been improved and newly designated as the Pine-Oak nature trail. To get there, follow the signs to Cades Cove Campground. Just before you arrive, you'll pass the picnic area and then the stables (closed in winter; see the chapter on horseback riding). Unless you're camping at Cades Cove, you'll have to park in the large lot behind the camp store, next to the ranger station, and walk a quarter mile down the campground road to the trailhead. You'll find it in section C, across from campsite 17. (This will actually make for a total hike of one mile.)

Feel free to use the restrooms behind the camp store.

Cosby
One mile roundtrip

This purely magical nature trail sits in the middle of the Cosby Campground (closed in winter; see the chapter on camping). To get there from the Sugarlands Visitor Center, drive east from Gatlinburg along Route 321, the northern boundary of the park. Turn right at the T-intersection in Cosby and follow Route 32 to the Cosby entrance to the park. Turn right again and proceed to the Cosby Picnic Area (see the chapter on picnicking) and then the check-in point for the campground. Park at the amphitheater. The trailhead is near the parking lot, by the bridge over Cosby Creek.

If ever there was a fairyland, surely this wooded nature trail hopping over the creek again and again must be it. The trail is certainly blessed with a profusion of wildflowers in the spring. But the moss-covered rocks, trees, and logs and the multiple miscellaneous fingers and rivulets of creek gurgling and bubbling over the river stone on both sides of the winding trail make it enchanting year-round.

You'll find plenty of odd-looking stilted or tented roots here. Can you figure out how they got this way? These yellow birch trees started out as seedlings on mossy old logs that had fallen on the forest floor. The young trees sent their roots down the sides of the fallen log. When the old log finally rotted away, the trees were left with stilted roots. You might also find a pile of stones that once was a chimney. You'll pass an old rock wall or two, and a spring where mountain folk got their water. Across the large bridge near the end, your kids will positively marvel at the hollowed-out stump with holes worn through it, filled with rocks.

Balsam Mountain
One mile roundtrip; closed in winter

The drive to get to this nature trail is a scenic trip in itself (see the chapter on scenic drives). From the Oconaluftee Visitor Center, take the Blue Ridge Parkway to milepost 458 and turn left at the big sign for Balsam Mountain onto Heintooga Ridge Road (closed in winter). The trailhead is eight miles up the road, just inside the entrance to the

Hen Wallow Falls in Cosby.

Balsam Mountain Campground (closed in winter; see the chapter on camping), next to site #44.

During summer, the blackberry bushes along this narrow path (through hardwoods at first and then evergreens) are brimming with sweet treats. This trail isn't a loop, and the end brings you out of the woods to a spot further up the road. You can either retrace your steps to return, or turn right onto the road and walk back to the campground that way.

Noah "Bud" Ogle Place
0.75 mile roundtrip

This historic nature trail (and one of the best wildflower walks in the spring) gives you a glimpse into what life on a mountain farm was like before the park was created. The trail begins at the Ogles' cabin, located on Cherokee Orchard Road, right before the start of the Roaring Fork Motor Nature Trail (see the chapter on scenic drives). Ogle belonged to one of the first families to settle in the community then known as White Oak Flats (now the bustling town of Gatlinburg). Noah and his wife, Cindy, lived here from 1883 until 1925.

Start by exploring the two-room log cabin. It may look rustic, but the Ogles had something many mountaineers didn't—running water. It flowed through a wooden trough from a nearby spring to a wooden sink on the back porch.

Then follow the trail through the woods to check out the remains of the "weaner" or honeymooner cabin. Newlyweds in the family lived here for a year or so until they could build a house of their own. Another highlight of this walk is the Ogles' tub mill, used to grind grain for the family as well as others in the community. The kids can do a little boulder hopping on the way to the last stop, the Ogles' barn.

Mingus Mill
closed in winter

Mingus Mill, on Newfound Gap Road (U.S. 441), just a half mile north of Oconaluftee Visitor Center, dates from 1886. This large, multi-story mill ground corn and wheat for more than 50 years before closing with the coming of the park. Renovated in 1968, the mill is now open for touring from mid-March through Thanksgiving weekend. (The paved and packed-gravel trail here is wheelchair accessible, with assistance.)

Don't be surprised if you don't see a waterwheel. There isn't one. Instead, the millstones do their work thanks to a water-powered, cast-iron turbine. To see the turbine, you can peer through the safety slats underneath the mill from the outside.

Inside the mill, the miller explains how the turbine and the mill operate and answers questions. You'll also find a few more exhibits on the second floor. You can buy stone-ground flour and cornmeal as well as a favorite old-fashioned mountaineer staple: lye soap!

Mingus Mill is one of three working mills in the park—the others are in Cades Cove and along Roaring Fork Motor Nature Trail.

Before you leave, follow the flume and the race (the stream of water in-between the moss-covered wooden boards) for 200 yards behind the mill to the small wooden dam in Mingus Creek.

Restrooms are located next to the parking lot (and include handicapped facilities).

Mingus Mill (left), where stone-ground cornmeal is made. Above, the historic barn on the grounds of the Mountain Farm Museum.

Mountain Farm Museum

The Mountain Farm Museum sits right next to the Oconaluftee Visitor Center (see the chapter on visitor centers), on the bank of the Oconaluftee River. Most of the buildings here date from around 1900 and weren't ever part of one farm. The Park Service moved them here from various other spots throughout the park in the early 1950s. (The paths here are hard-packed and gravel, making it wheelchair accessible, with assistance.)

What makes the Mountain Farm Museum different is that it's an actual working farm. Vegetables are growing in the garden, and there's real corn in the cornfield. The apple trees are carefully tended. Hens scurry about the property, roosters crow, and hogs grunt from their pen.

The log cabin you'll see, the Davis House, is fully furnished. The volunteers in period dress point out an unusual element in the home's construction—the chestnut logs that the cabin is made of were split in half and placed in matching positions on opposite walls, so that the walls that face each other are like mirror images of each other.

Other buildings on the farmstead include a chicken house, a sorghum mill for making sorghum molasses, corn cribs, a meathouse for

On a Saturday in late September each year, Oconaluftee celebrates the annual Mountain Life Festival. The event is free and lasts all day long. Park volunteers demonstrate how to make sorghum molasses, apple butter, hominy, apple cider, and even lye soap. Kids can also watch how to make traditional mountain toys. Adding to the festive air is traditional live music.

It takes more than 16,000 wooden shingles to re-roof the barn at the Mountain Farm Museum.

smoking pork, an ash hopper to store the wood ashes used to make lye soap, a woodshed, a blacksmith's shop for repairing tools, a springhouse to keep perishable foods cold, a bee gum stand for collecting honey, and a huge barn (the only building original to the site) filled with various farm tools and equipment. The apple house once stored apples for making cider, vinegar, and apple butter. There's even an outhouse with a Plexiglas front so you can open the door to see (but not pee) inside!

The trailhead for the Oconaluftee River Trail (three miles roundtrip; see the chapter on other family-fun hikes) begins here, as well. You'll find restrooms at the visitor center.

Quiet Walkways

As you drive on the park's roads, you'll probably see several small signs that say "Quiet Walkway" sprinkled about here and there. Each of these gems offers a quarter-mile to a half-mile fairly level and easy trail that meanders back into the woods and away from the road. There's no real destination—it's just a chance to get away from it all. Walk as far as you want, and then turn around and return the way you came. (A few loop back, but most of them do not.)

You'll note that there are only a few parking spots at each Quiet Walkway, ensuring that they can't get crowded. These tiny trails are a great way to get a taste of what it's like being in the woods and surrounded by nature if you have limited time or energy. They're also a great way to fit another short hike into a day of exploring the park!

SMOKIES WORD SEARCH

Using any park guide, complete the names for these places in the park. After you fill in the blanks for each place, then find it on a park map.

S _ g _ _ _ l _ _ nds

_ li _ g _ an _ D _ _ _ e

Sm _ k _ m _ n _

D _ ep _ _ re _ k

N _ _ f _ _ _ nd _ _ _ p

_ o _ th _ l _ s P _ r _ _ _ a _

_ a _ es _ ov _

C _ t _ lo _ c _ e _

O _ on _ l _ f _ _ _ e

_ oo _ R _ _ _ k

A _ _ _ a _ a _ _ _ ia _ T _ a _ l

R _ ar _ ng _ or _

_ ot _ r _ a _ ur _ T _ a _ l

_ al _ am M _ un _ a _ n

_ os _ y

B _ _ _ C _ ee _

A _ ra _ _ s C _ e _ k

CHAPTER 10

Waterfall Hikes & Walks

Of all the 800 miles of hiking trails in the national park, perhaps the most popular and fun are the many waterfalls trails. With the highest elevations in the Smokies getting enough rain to qualify as a rainforest, there's enough of the wet stuff here to feed 2,115 miles of streams, allowing these mountains to be fairly generous with the waterworks. Fortunately for families, many of the most beautiful falls are not all that hard to get to.

Do heed the warning signs and make sure your kids don't climb on the wet rocks next to or in the falls, no matter how harmless it may seem. They're much slipperier than they look, and many people who have tried have been seriously injured (or worse). As tempting as it may be to take a dip, don't swim here either. The pools at many of the falls have strong undertows, and people have drowned.

By the way, you might consider repeating these hikes during future visits, because the appearance of the falls changes with the rainfall. In general, the best months for waterfalls are March and July, when the Smokies get the most rain. (September and October are the driest months.)

What follows are descriptions of the best waterfall hikes for families, starting with the easiest and getting progressively more difficult. Then, you'll read about a few falls you can enjoy without even having to hike.

For an encore: Yet another waterfall hike to Indian Flats Falls (7.5 miles roundtrip; moderate) along the Middle Prong Trail in Tremont is included in the chapter on other family-fun hikes. It's described as an option in the section about the Old Cadillac hike.

Cataract Falls
0.7 mile roundtrip; easy

If your kids are too small for a big hike, then this is the waterfall hike for you. The walk is short and mostly flat, and the trailhead is right behind the Sugarlands Visitor Center. To get there from the visitor center, pass the restrooms and start out on the **Fighting Creek Self-Guiding**

Nature Trail (see the chapter on self-guiding nature trails).

After the long bridge, the trail forks. The nature trail goes left, but you'll take the trail going right to Cataract Falls. On the way to the falls, you go through a short tunnel under a road and cross the stream on some rocks (a good salamander spot). The 40-foot cascade is a short walk from here.

Three Waterfalls Loop: Juney Whank Falls, Indian Creek Falls, & Tom Branch Falls
2.4 miles roundtrip; easy to moderate

Why see one waterfall when you can have a triple treat? Deep Creek features three splendid, easy-to-reach falls that are easy to combine into one hike, unofficially called the **Three Waterfalls Loop**. (Think of it as a hat trick for your hiking boots.) More good news: you'll be able to see blooms most of the year here—wildflowers dot the woods in the spring, rhododendron and mountain laurel show off in the summer, and several fall flowers grace the area in early autumn.

To get to Deep Creek, drive to Bryson City and follow the signs in town that lead to the Deep Creek Campground and Picnic Area. Drive past the turnoff to the campground (closed in winter; see the chapter on camping)—do not cross the bridge on the right. Then pass the picnic area (see the chapter on picnicking) that's immediately after that. Park at the end of the road in the large parking lot, where you'll find the trailheads for both the **Juney Whank Falls Trail** and the **Deep Creek Trail**.

(Please note: There's an official trail in Deep Creek called the Loop Trail. This is *not* the same as the Three Waterfalls Loop described here, which is not signed as such. If you follow the directions below closely, you shouldn't get confused or lost.)

Start at the sign for the Juney Whank Falls Trail. The start of the trail includes a steep uphill section, but worry not. This isn't a difficult hike.

Keep following the signs to the falls, and before long you'll take a very short side trail off to the right that leads to a lovely little wooden footbridge (complete with bench) crossing Juney Whank Branch in the middle of the 90-foot falls. Above the bridge is the 40-foot upper falls, while below the bridge is the 50-foot lower falls—so don't forget to look downstream, as well.

Then continue across the bridge and on the path up the bank. At the top, turn right to get back onto the horse trail. (In a short while, there's a sign at a cutoff on the right that goes downhill to the Deep Creek Trail. This is actually the continuation of the Juney Whank Falls

FUN factivity

On your way back from Cataract Falls, check out Lower Fighting Creek Cemetery. It's on top of a small rise at the corner of the road behind Park Service headquarters. Find the large monument with "Evans" carved into it. This stone marks the burial place for Richard Evans (known as Preacher Dick), the first pastor of the Evans Chapel Church, which once stood near here. Reverend Evans and his wife had 11 daughters.

FUN fact

Both Juney Whank Branch and Juney Whank Falls were named for a man named Junaluska ("Juney" for short) Whank, who is said to be buried near the falls. The phrase Juney Whank is also a Cherokee name for "Place where the bear passes."

Trail—although it's not marked as such—so take it if you want to return to the parking lot. To see the other falls, ignore this and bear left, staying on the horse trail.)

You'll next walk uphill for about a half mile, and then you'll descend to a sharp hairpin turn by a bubbly creek called **Hammer Branch** that the trail follows for a bit. Where the horse trail dead ends, turn right (downhill) onto the Deep Creek Trail. You'll soon cross two very wide wooden bridges fairly close together that take you over Deep Creek and then Indian Creek.

Immediately after the second bridge, turn left onto the **Indian Creek Trail**, another wide, gravel trail. You'll see a sign announcing that the falls are in 200 feet. After you've walked that far, you'll see a log bench and another sign to the left of the trail, pointing the way to the falls down the bank. Walk this way to see 45-foot **Indian Creek Falls**, a pretty little cascade over a slanted rock face.

After you've seen the falls, retrace your steps to get back to where you left the Deep Creek Trail, just after the second wide wooden bridge. Now turn left onto the Deep Creek Trail, following the sign pointing the way to the trailhead. In a half mile, you'll see 80-foot **Tom Branch Falls** on the left side of the trail and across Deep Creek. Five benches face the falls, offering a great place to admire the view. In 0.2 mile, you'll be back at the parking lot.

***Shorter options*:** You can also hike just to **Juney Whank Fall**s on the Juney Whank Falls Trail (0.6 mile roundtrip; easy to moderate) or to just Tom Branch Falls on the Deep Creek Trail (0.5 mile roundtrip; easy).

To hike to Indian Creek Falls (1.6 miles roundtrip; easy), start out on the Deep Creek Trail. You'll see Tom Branch Falls on the right after just 0.2 mile. In another half a mile, turn right onto the Indian

Tom Branch Falls.

Creek Trail and go only about 200 feet to Indian Creek Falls. Then backtrack the way you came. The elevation gain for this hike is a mere 100 feet, so it's about as easy as they come.

To combine Juney Whank and Tom Branch falls (about one mile roundtrip; easy to moderate), start out on the Juney Whank Falls Trail to the falls. Soon after the falls, follow the sign on the right at the cut-off that descends to the Deep Creek Trail. Turn left onto the Deep Creek Trail and walk only about 50 yards or so to Tom Branch Falls, which will be on the right. Then backtrack on the Deep Creek Trail, following it 0.2 mile to the parking lot.

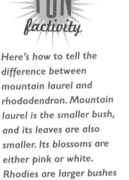

Here's how to tell the difference between mountain laurel and rhododendron. Mountain laurel is the smaller bush, and its leaves are also smaller. Its blossoms are either pink or white. Rhodies are larger bushes with larger leaves, and their flowers are white, purple, or just about any shade of pinkish-purple in-between. See if you can find examples of each. Do you notice a difference in where each grows? Laurel prefers drier soil, while rhododendrons grow where it's damper.

Laurel Falls
2.6 miles roundtrip; easy

The **Laurel Falls Trail** enjoys the distinction of being the only trail in the Smokies that's paved (if you don't count the shorter Sugarlands Valley or Clingmans Dome self-guiding nature trails). You can take a stroller up this one (but it is too rough and steep for most wheelchair users). The paving, the short length, and the mere 300-foot elevation gain make it an easier outing than most Smoky Mountain trails.

This is one of the park's self-guiding nature trails, so be sure to use the guide booklet available for a small fee from the visitor centers or on the honor system from the box at the trailhead.

The stream, **Laurel Branch**, and the 85-foot-high Laurel Falls are appropriately named—mountain laurel (as well as rhododendron) grows all along this trail, blooming in May. You'll walk through both a pine-oak forest as well as a cove hardwood forest on your way. The falls is actually in two segments, and the trail crosses the water on the ledge between the two, so don't forget to look downstream from the falls, as well. After the falls, the trail continues (although unpaved) another three miles to the crest of Cove Mountain—a steeper segment not described here.

To get to the trailhead, drive 3.8 miles from the Sugarlands Visitor Center down Little River Road (toward Cades Cove). Parking is on both sides of the road here. The trail is so popular that at times the parking lot is completely full (especially during summer). If you visit in high season, you may want to plan your hike for the morning for this reason.

Grotto Falls
2.4 miles roundtrip; moderate

The fun factor for this waterfall hike (via the **Trillium Gap Trail**) is pretty high because Grotto Falls is the only falls in the park where the trail lets you walk behind the waterfall. The elevation gain is only 560 feet, so it's fairly manageable for most families. The trail takes you through a forest of impressive old-growth hemlock trees and crosses

Laurel Falls.

the water several times on its way, finally arriving at the 25-foot falls. (You will get a little wet from the spray as you walk behind the falls, but in the summer it feels good!) Around the edges of the pool at the base of the falls is a favorite place to find salamanders.

The Trillium Gap Trail continues past the falls (and gets steeper) for an additional 5.3 miles, going all the way to the summit of **Mount Le Conte** (which would make the total hike 13 miles roundtrip, bumping up the rating to difficult).

On Mondays, Wednesdays, and Fridays in the summer, you might encounter llamas on the Trillium Gap Trail as they take supplies up to Le Conte Lodge (see the chapter on hikes with a view), which is only accessible by foot. Llamas are the perfect pack animal because their relatively soft hooves do the least amount of damage to the trails.

To get to the trailhead, turn at traffic light #8 in Gatlinburg and follow Historic Nature Trail/Airport Road to Cherokee Orchard Road and then on to the Roaring Fork Motor Nature Trail (closed in winter; see the chapter on scenic drives). Park in the lot at marker #5. Restrooms (vault toilets) are available near the trailhead.

To hike to Grotto Falls in winter, when Roaring Fork Motor Nature Trail is closed, drive as far as you can on Cherokee Orchard Road and park in the lot by the Rainbow Falls/Bull Head trailhead. Then walk two miles down the motor nature trail to the Trillium Gap trailhead. This option brings your total mileage for this hike to 6.4 miles.

Hen Wallow Falls
4.4 miles roundtrip; moderate

Hen Wallow Falls, at 95 feet, is one of the highest waterfalls in the park. The trail that takes you there, the **Gabes Mountain Trail**, travels through hemlock trees and rhododendron thickets, and for part of the way it follows an old roadbed. (If you look, you can even see the remains of a few homesteads off to the side.) You'll cross the creek on rocks in a few places, and at the end you take a steep cut-off trail downhill about 800 feet to the base of the falls. At the bottom, right before you get to the falls, look for the unusual large crystal rocks.

Do you know the difference between a waterfall and a cascade? A waterfall is when water falls straight down over a cliff, without hitting rocks along the way that divert its flow. A cascade isn't quite as direct—the water hits rocks or ledges before it hits the pool below. Some waterfalls are actually both!

The falls start out narrow (the creek at the top is only two feet wide), but as they spill over the cliff, they bounce onto a large rock that bulges out near the bottom, fanning the water out to about 20 feet at the base. This is an excellent spot for salamander sightings. The elevation gain for this hike is a respectable 520 feet.

To get to the trailhead, drive about 19 miles east of Gatlinburg on Route 321 along the northern border of the park. Turn right at the T-intersection in Cosby and follow Route 32 to the Cosby entrance to the national park. Drive two miles to the Cosby Picnic Area (see the chapter on picnicking), near the entrance to the Cosby Campground (closed in winter; see the chapter on camping), and park in the designated hiker parking area. Then backtrack on foot about 100 yards along the main road to the trailhead for the Gabes Mountain Trail. If you're camping at the Cosby Campground, you can take the short access trail near campsite A-45 instead.

The trailhead for the Cosby Self-guiding Nature Trail (one mile roundtrip; see the chapter on self-guiding nature trails) is next to the

Rainbow Falls.

amphitheater in the campground, and the Foothills Parkways East is about eight miles away.

Abrams Falls
5 miles roundtrip; moderate

These falls are only 25 feet high, but don't let their small stature fool you—they boast the biggest volume in the park. The sheer force of the water flowing over this ledge, the roar the falls make, and the mist they kick up are all impressive. (In fact, you may be able to see a rainbow in the mist if you arrive on a sunny morning.)

The lovely pool at the base of the falls is 100 feet across, one of the largest natural pools in the park. (Definitely don't swim here—it may be enticing, but the undertow is *very* dangerous and people have drowned.) The mountain laurel you'll hike through on the way up makes this a particularly pretty hike in late May. The elevation gain is a relatively modest 340 feet.

The trailhead is on the Cades Cove Loop Road (see the chapter on scenic drives), down the half-mile gravel road leading to the Elijah Oliver place (about halfway through the loop and the last stop before the Cades Cove Visitor Center). Traffic on the loop drive can be heavy in peak season, so plan accordingly.

Abrams Falls (and Abrams Creek) were named for a Cherokee chief whose village once stood several miles downstream. His wife, Kate, may be for whom Cades Cove was named.

Rainbow Falls
5.4 miles roundtrip; moderate to difficult

On sunny afternoons, you may be able to see why these falls got their name—if conditions are right, a rainbow forms in the mist from the 75-foot waterfall. This hike shows off wildflowers in the spring and impressive ice formations during extended periods of winter cold when both the bottom and the top freeze. (Take extra care at this time of year, because the rocks and bridge by the falls may be icy.)

You'll see a smaller eight-foot waterfall on this hike, too—just before the main event. Very soon after these minor falls, you'll cross two footbridges that offer a lovely view of the larger falls (unless the leaves block the view in summer).

This trail is on the steep side, with an elevation gain of 1,500 feet. If your kids are particularly hardy hikers, you might consider continuing on the trail another four miles to the summit of Mount Le Conte (for a total of 13.4 miles roundtrip), but allow plenty of time if you do.

To get to the trailhead, turn at traffic light #8 in Gatlinburg and follow Historic Nature Trail/Airport Road to Cherokee Orchard Road and the entrance to the national park. Park at the lot just past the Noah "Bud" Ogle homesite (0.75 mile roundtrip; see the chapter on self-guiding nature trails). Roaring Fork Motor Nature Trail (closed in winter) is just beyond this parking lot. Restrooms (vault toilets) are available near the trailhead.

Mingo Falls.

WATERFALLS YOU CAN DRIVE TO

MINGO FALLS: One of the tallest falls in the southern Appalachians, this 180-foot waterfall is actually not in the national park but is instead in the adjacent Cherokee reservation. Splashing over hundreds of small shelves, the falls look something like liquid lace.

To get there from Oconaluftee Visitor Center, drive south on U.S. 441 for 2.5 miles and turn onto Big Cove Road. Go about five miles, and then turn right at the sign for Mingo Falls Campground. Drive over a short bridge and park in the lot. Then take the short trail (a quarter of a mile each way) with many steps to the base of the falls. Alternatively, you could take the Balsam Mountain Loop scenic drive (see the chapter on scenic drives), which includes Mingo Falls near the end.

PLACE OF A THOU-SAND DRIPS: This 80-foot waterfall must really be magic, because it appears and disappears. During dry spells, you'd drive right past it without a second glance. But after a hard rain, the water runs over this rock face every which way in countless dramatic rivulets, some dropping as much as 20 feet, giving it its name. You'll find it at the very end of the Roaring Fork Motor Nature Trail (closed in winter; see the chapter on scenic drives), on the left at marker #15.

MEIGS FALLS: This pretty little 28-foot waterfall is tucked 300 feet back from the road. In the summer when the leaves are out, it isn't immediately obvious, so you have to look closely to see it. You'll find it along Little River Road (see the chapter on scenic drives) at marker #6, about 13 miles from the Sugarlands Visitor Center (or 4.6 miles from the Townsend "Y" near the Townsend entrance to the park). It's on the opposite side of the river at a longer-than-usual pullout that has a low stone wall.

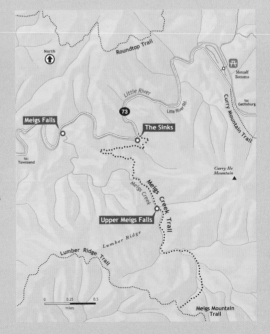

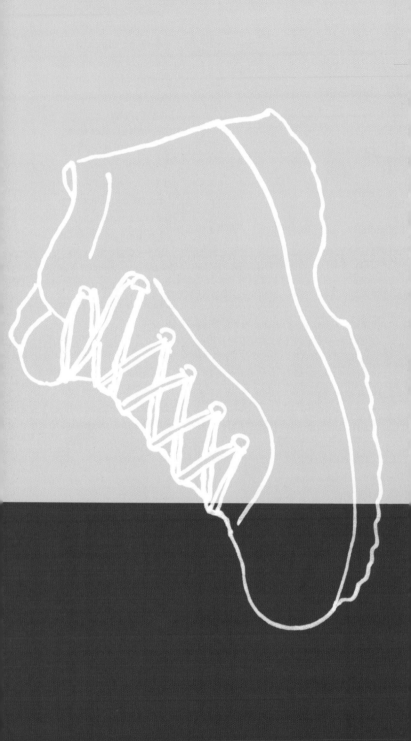

CHAPTER 11

Hikes & Walks With a View

The Smokies are hardly stingy when it comes to vistas. They're everywhere you look, it seems—including the many pull-offs on Newfound Gap Road (U.S. 441), the Foothills Parkway (East and West), and Heintooga Ridge Road on Balsam Mountain. But there's something quite satisfying about *hiking* with your family to a spot with an incredible view instead of the kids just climbing out of the car to see it. Somehow, when you feel you've earned it, the experience is sweeter.

FUN *fact*

Great Smoky Mountains National Park has 16 peaks above 6,000 feet.

What follows are four five-star, family-friendly views arranged in order from the easiest to the more difficult. *Bon altitude!*

Look Rock Tower Trail
One mile roundtrip; easy

One of the best-kept secrets in the Smokies is that you can get a 360-degree view arguably as fine as the one from Clingmans Dome but with far fewer people and a less steep walk—at the **Look Rock tower**. While the 2,670-foot elevation here is relatively modest as vistas go, the views are nonetheless impressive.

The trailhead is located at about the midpoint (and highest point) of the Foothills Parkway West (see the chapter on scenic drives). You'll no doubt be impressed at the overlook from the parking lot first, but that's just the beginning. Follow the paved path from the end of the parking lot that's nearest the campground (which you probably passed on the way in, if you came from the Townsend end as most people do). The path crosses the parkway and then heads uphill and into the woods.

At the top of the hill, the path deadends at a wider one-lane roadway (that's

FUN *factivity*

To view the data collected at the weather and air quality station you'll pass on the way to the tower at Look Rock, go online and visit www.nature.nps.gov/air/webcams/parks/grsmcam/grsmcam.cfm. The site also has a webcam, so you can enjoy the view any time you want (except after dark, of course)!

The spruce-fir forest.

FUN fact

The Cherokee called Clingmans Dome Kuwahi, meaning "mulberry place." It is considered sacred to members of the tribe even today. Cherokee legend says bears lived inside Clingmans Dome and held dances here every fall before hibernating.

closed to traffic). Turn left onto the roadway, and you'll soon pass a weather and air quality station on the right. Not far after that is the tower, with three segments of concrete ramp zigzagging up to the observation platform.

The view from one side of the observation platform is of Maryville, eight miles away, and Knoxville, 25 miles to the northwest. The southeast side has a mountainous view of the western side of the park, and directly in front of you is a pretty view of the pastoral parkway itself winding through the trees along the ridgeline. This view is especially marvelous in the fall when the leaves change color, and it's a favorite at sunset anytime.

Nearby are both the **Look Rock Campground** (closed in winter) and the **Look Rock Picnic Area** (closed in winter; see the chapter on picnicking). You can also begin this hike from the Look Rock Picnic Area (two miles roundtrip).

Clingmans Dome
One mile roundtrip; moderate;
access road closed to cars in winter

At 6,643 feet in elevation, Clingmans Dome is the highest point in the park—and many affectionately refer to it as "the top of ol' Smoky."

It's four times higher than the Empire State Building in New York City. In fact, Clingmans Dome is the highest point in the entire state of Tennessee. (It's also the highest point along the Appalachian Trail and the third highest mountain in the East.)

But getting to this lofty spot hardly requires a long, arduous hike. You can actually drive to within a half mile of the summit and walk the rest of the way on a wide, paved (but steep) walking path.

The trailhead is located at the parking lot at the end of Clingmans Dome Road (closed in winter). By the way, this walk is one of the park's self-guiding nature trails, so be sure to pick up the guide booklet for a nominal charge at one of the visitor centers or on the honor system from the box at the trailhead. You'll find an information center with publications and provisions for sale and park staff on hand to answer questions in the stone building just up the trail. The restrooms (vault toilets) are located beside the parking area.

FUN fact

Snow sometimes falls at Clingmans Dome as late as May and as early as October.

This paved trail is stroller-worthy but much too steep for most wheelchair users. In a half mile, it gains 330 feet in elevation with many benches along the way for resting. At the end of the walk, you'll ascend a 375-foot concrete spiral ramp (with a 12-percent grade) to the top of a 45-foot observation tower. This is a popular spot any time of day, but especially so at sunset.

When the weather is clear, the 360-degree panorama is simply stunning—you can see as far as 100 miles away, including parts of seven states. Clear weather is the exception rather than the rule, however, because this part of the park is practically a rainforest!

Unfortunately, air pollution also reduces visibility. In fact, in the last half of the 20th century, pollution was responsible for reducing the view from Clingmans Dome by as much as 40 percent in the winter and 80 percent in the summer. The main cause of the pollution is sulfates given off by coal-burning power plants from as far away as Indiana, Mississippi, and Missouri. However, air quality is getting better, thanks to a number of different factors. The good news is that visibility has begun to improve in the past decade!

This part of the park is in the **spruce-fir forest**, one of the few places in the world where the Fraser fir tree grows wild. Christmas tree farms in many other places often plant Frasers, but they are native only in some of the highest elevations in North Carolina, Tennessee, and Virginia.

FUN fact

The Civilian Conservation Corps originally built Clingmans Dome tower out of wood in 1935. The Park Service constructed the present-day concrete and steel tower in 1960.

Unfortunately, most of the park's Frasers have been killed by a non-native insect pest called the **balsam woolly adelgid** (see the chapter on trees, balds, and wildflowers).

To see Clingmans Dome in winter, when the road is closed, you could hike the seven miles each way from the Newfound Gap parking lot, but that would make your total hike to the tower and back 15 miles—too much for most families. However, if your family enjoys cross-country skiing or snow shoeing and you have your own equipment, bounding along the closed road to the trailhead can be an excellent option. (Or you could just wander

FUN *factivity*

down the road part way and let the kids build snowmen or make snow angels—this is one of the snowiest places you'll find in the park.) All of this assumes there actually is snow in the park's high country, which is probably so less than half the period the road is closed, from December 1 - March 31.

Nearby, you'll find the trailhead for the Forney Ridge Trail, which leads to Andrews Bald (3.6 miles roundtrip; described next).

Andrews Bald
3.6 miles roundtrip; moderate; access road closed to cars in winter

The most easily accessible of the park's balds, Andrews Bald (elevation 5,860 feet) is the highest bald in the Smokies (see the chapter on trees, balds and wildflowers). The trail is extremely rocky in spots, especially at the beginning, but because it starts at a high elevation, there's not much climb to it, so it shouldn't entail too much huffing and puffing.

Because of the elevation, the weather here is cooler and windier than on many other trails in the park, so it's especially important to be prepared with jackets or sweaters.

FUN *fact*

To get to the bald, first drive to the parking lot at the end of Clingmans Dome Road (closed in winter). Start your hike at the trailhead for the **Forney Ridge Trail**, just before the start of the Clingmans Dome Self-Guiding Nature Trail (one mile roundtrip; described above).

Although you'll see many dead Fraser firs in this area, you'll no doubt still be able to smell their wonderful scent. At the start of this trail, note the unusual natural rings on the boulders (see the Fun Factivity, above). In July and August, you're likely to find ripe blackberries and raspberries along the way. Definitely enjoy them, but check them for stinkbugs before you pop any into your mouth.

Andrews Bald was named for Andres Thompson, a mountaineer (and later a Civil War soldier) who moved his family to the bald in 1850, after having herded cattle to the bald for several years previously.

When you get to the bald, you'll find big boulders strewn about, various bushes, and plenty of wild oat grass everywhere. Have fun exploring the entire area. The best vistas can be had at the higher spots of the field, where in some places the views surround you on three sides.

In late spring and early summer, you'll see Catawba rhododendron blooming at the top of the bald as you enter it from the trail; down the hill, the flame azalea will be in all its glory. By the end of August and in early September, you're likely to find tall blueberry bushes loaded with fruit (unless the bears have gotten to them first). In autumn, look for fall wildflowers to bloom profusely.

Alum Cave Trail to Mount Le Conte
11 miles roundtrip; difficult

This popular trail starts on **Newfound Gap Road** (U.S. 441), nine miles from the Sugarlands Visitor Center. With an elevation gain of 2,600 feet, this is the shortest and steepest of the five hiking trails to 6,593-foot Mount Le Conte (the third-highest peak in the Smokies). This trail is also excellent for rhododendron in early June.

The first part of this hike, to **Alum Cave Bluff**, is one of the park's self-guiding nature trails, although unlike the others, this one doesn't have numbered posts. Pick up the guide booklet for a nominal charge at one of the visitor centers or on the honor system from the box at the trailhead.

The trail starts out following **Alum Cave Creek**, a good place to search for salamanders. After 1.5 miles, you'll reach **Arch Rock**, a natural stone arch carved by the freeze and thaw of water. The trail actually climbs through the arch on stone steps. (By the way, if you turn around at Arch Rock, your roundtrip hike would be three miles.) After the arch, the trail hits its first fairly steep section, and at one point you'll see the first of several sets of steel cables anchored to the rock face to make the going easier when there's ice.

One mile from Arch Rock, you reach Alum Cave Bluffs, which is not really a cave but a rock overhang. You'll immediately notice the musty, sulfur-like smell in the air here, coming from the minerals in the rock. For a very short time, the 100-foot-high bluffs were mined for Epsom salts and "pseudo-alum," and legend has it that hundreds of Confederate soldiers extracted saltpeter for gunpowder from them

Alum Cave Bluffs.

during the Civil War. (By the way, if you turned back from here, your roundtrip hike would be five miles, with an elevation gain of 1,160 feet.)

From this point, it's only three more miles to the top of **Mount Le Conte**, although the going is rather steep, including quite a climb on a set of log stairs. When you reach the junction with the **Rainbow Falls Trail**, you'll know you're within shouting distance of **Le Conte Lodge** (the highest-elevation guest lodge in the eastern U.S.), just below the summit proper of 6,593-foot Mount Le Conte.

In addition to the Alum Cave Trail, the four other trails to Mount Le Conte include the Rainbow Falls Trail (13.4 miles roundtrip; see the chapter on waterfalls hikes); the Trillium Gap Trail, including Grotto Falls (17.8 miles roundtrip; see the chapter on waterfall hikes); the Boulevard Trail (16.2 miles roundtrip, including a short stretch on the Appalachian Trail to get to where the Boulevard Trail begins); and the Bull Head Trail (13 miles roundtrip, including a short stretch on the Old Sugarlands Trail to get to where the Bull Head Trail begins).

Even if you're not staying overnight at the lodge, you can use the restrooms as well as buy snacks (such as baked goods, candy bars, soda, coffee, lemonade, and hot chocolate), in addition to Mount Le Conte shirts, hats, hiking sticks, water bottles, medallions, bandanas, patches, and postcards as well as batteries, film, disposable cameras, trail maps, and trail guides (cash or check only; no credit cards at the lodge). As of 2011, you can even buy a bag lunch or, if you have reservations, a simple but hot and hearty lunch in the dining room.

Staying overnight at Le Conte Lodge: This lodge at the summit of Mount Le Conte is accessible only via hiking trail. The complex consists of the rustic main lodge (built in 1926) plus a dining lodge and 10 cabins that can house a maximum of 60 guests.

The rough-hewn cabins include seven one-room private cabins with bunk beds that sleep four to five people each, as well as three group cabins with either two or three private bedrooms and a shared living room. All the cabins have tables and chairs, as well as covered porches with rocking chairs. There's no electricity or running water in the sleeping quarters, but there are flush toilets in a separate building, and each cabin is equipped with kerosene lanterns, propane heaters, and a washbasin and bucket. The lodge provides all linens (including sheets, wool blankets, pillows, and pillowcases).

Jack Huff, who for many years operated the lodge atop Mount Le Conte, carried his ailing mother up the mountain in a chair he strapped to his back. Find the picture of Jack carrying his mother on the chair in the lodge building.

You need to bring hand towels, washcloths, your own toiletries (although the lodge does sell toothbrushes, in case you forgot yours), and a flashlight. Pack a sweater or jacket, even in July. Nights can be cold, even in the summer, when a low of 35 degrees is not unheard of. During spring and fall, the low can even

Le Conte Lodge is accessible only via hiking trail.

About 63,000 hikers climb to the top of Mount Le Conte every year. About 13,000 of them stay overnight in Le Conte Lodge.

hit the teens—with snow! Daytime highs, by the way, have never reached 80 degrees.

The overnight fee includes both dinner and breakfast (as well as lunch if you're staying more than one night), served family-style in the dining lodge. Adults can even buy wine with dinner.

Guests mingle at the main lodge, where you can borrow books and games and sit on rocking chairs on the deck when it's warm.

Two short trails from the lodge with fabulous views are traditions with guests—the quarter-mile trail to Cliff Tops (a treeless, rocky ledge) for sunset and the mile-long trail to the Myrtle Point Overlook for sunrise.

Le Conte Lodge operates only from late March through late November, and reservations are required (call 1-865-429-5704 or visit *www.leconte-lodge.com*). Be forewarned that the lodge begins taking reservations in October for the following season, and most dates are taken already by November. So plan ahead if you want to stay here!

CHAPTER 12

Other Family-Fun Hikes

This chapter presents a grab bag of miscellaneous family-fun hikes, each with its own charm. Some lead to urban areas and allow you to take your dog along, quite a few give you a taste of history (allowing you to explore old homesteads, cemeteries, a schoolhouse, and even an old rusting car), and one takes you on a bit of the famous Appalachian Trail. Many are blessed with still more waterfalls. They're presented here roughly in order of the easiest to the more difficult.

The Gatlinburg Trail
Two miles one-way, or four miles roundtrip; easy

Although this trail is officially called the Gatlinburg Trail, it's also sometimes referred to as the Two-Mile Trail. But they are both the same thing—a wide, flat walk beside a stretch of streambed between the Sugarlands Visitor Center (see the chapter on visitor centers) and downtown Gatlinburg.

If you have two vehicles, you might consider leaving one at the end of your walk, making this a two-mile, one-way excursion. Alternately, if you're staying in Gatlinburg and you're here between June and October, you could hike this trail one-way to the Sugarlands Visitor Center and from there, for a small fee, catch the Gatlinburg trolley (see the shuttle bus section of the chapter on what families need to know) back to town. The trolley also stops at the trailhead for the Laurel Falls Trail and the Elkmont Campground before returning to Gatlinburg, so you'd get a bit of a scenic tour down Little River Road, as well. (Although Pigeon Forge and Sevierville also have trolley service, their trolleys do not go into the national park.)

This is one of two trails in the park where you can walk your dog (the other one is the Oconaluftee River Trail, described next). However, please note that your pet must be on a leash that's no longer than six feet. Also be sure to bring bags to pick up any pet waste.

You can also ride a bike on this trail, and you might be able to take a stroller or trail-ready wheelchair along this route.

You can, of course, hike this in either direction. But this description starts from Gatlinburg at the trailhead on River Road by the city

How the World Was Made

Cherokees attach a special meaning to the buzzards that you often see circling over these mountains and valleys.

A long time ago, there were only two people and the animals. And they all lived together on a tiny little rock in the middle of the water. There was no more room on the rock, so the animals decided they would dive down in the water and try to find some more land. Mr. Turtle said, "Maybe I can find some more land." So he dove down. When he returned, on the bottom of all four of his feet there was some mud. And they carefully got all the mud off, and they laid it out on the rocks. And when it was dry enough, Grandfather threw mud out into the water, and it became land.

It was very soft and muddy. And the buzzard flew with his great wings, and said, "With the air from my wings, I'll make a fan and dry it." But each time when his wings went down, it would make a big valley, and each time the wings would go up, it would make a big mountain. And today, when you look all around us, what do we have here? Mountains where his wings went up and made the mountains and valleys when they went down.

Adapted from Kathi Smith Littlejohn, "How the World Was Made,"
Living Stories of the Cherokee

Buzzard soaring over mountains, by Cherokee

One of the bilingual storyboards along the Oconaluftee River Trail.

waterworks building. A crushed gravel path follows the West Prong of the Little Pigeon River here, and almost immediately you'll see an old stone wall on your left. The path goes over a footbridge and through the woods, and before long you'll pass what's left of two chimneys (an older-looking stone one and a more modern one) that may have belonged to some summer homes that were here before the park was established.

A little further on the right, you'll find some semi-circular steps that no longer lead anywhere but into the woods. After you walk under an overpass (the Gatlinburg bypass that takes drivers from Pigeon Forge directly into the park), you'll see a cascade on the left.

In about a quarter mile, the path passes the park's maintenance sheds, but if you hike this way in the fall, concentrate instead on the colorful leaves on the ridge behind the sheds. Here, the path gets a bit less distinct (although, actually, more concrete) because from here you walk along a road for park vehicles before passing the park headquarters building.

At the corner of the road leading to the parking area for the headquarters building, you may want to explore the small cemetery you see among the trees on the rise (see the description of this cemetery in the section on Cataract Falls in the chapter on waterfall hikes).

After passing the park headquarters, you'll also pass the trailhead for the **Fighting Creek Self-Guiding Nature Trail** (one mile roundtrip; see the chapter on self-guiding nature trails). This is also the way to **Cataract Falls** (0.7 mile roundtrip). The path then leads past restrooms and a vending machine area, and around the corner to the left is the entrance to the Sugarlands Visitor Center.

ᏇᎣᎵᎢ ᏪᏟᎭ ᏇᏆᎤᏭᏓ

Ꭴ ᎿᏆ ᏓᎠᎢ ᏞᏞᏆᎣᏗᏳᏔ Ꭴ ᏗᏞᏟᏬᎩ ᏲᏛᏇᎢ ᏝᏞ.

ᏣᎥᏴ Ꭴ ᏟᏌᎵ ᏓᏝ~ᏴᎵ ᏟᎶᏟᏳ ᏭᏁ ᏔᏌᏂ ᏴᎡ ᏓᏟ
ᏔᎤᎵ ᏓᎤ. Ꮣ4Ꮓ Ꭴ ᏓᏝ~ ᏓᏴᎵ ᏟᏬᎤ ᏚᏬᎤᎶᏓᎬ
ᏓᏟ ᏔᎤᎵ ᏚᏟᎠᏬᏟ ᏲᏳᏟᎤᏝ ᏓᏝ~Ꮝ ᏪᎵᏟ
ᏝᏌᏬᎤᏔ. ᏝᏚᎦ ᏚᏟᏝᏞ, ᏓᎤᎤ ᏓᏚ ᏮᏠᏞᏓ ᏴᎵᎵ
ᏢᏛᏟ. ᏓᏚ ᏲᏚᏟᏟ ᏓᏟ ᏲᎷᏗ ᏞᏚᎵ ᏚᏪᏞᏚᎵ ᏴᏟᏗ
ᏗᏝᏞᎢ. ᏝᏟᏟᏚᏆ ᏚᏪᏞᏚᎵ ᏚᏆᏟᏟ ᏟᏬ ᏳᎷᏟᎤ ᏴᏟᏗ.
ᏲᏴᏃᏬ ᎢᏴ ᏚᏚᏞ ᏴᏟᏗ ᏝᏟᏯᏟ ᏓᏝ~Ꮭ ᏓᏟ ᏚᏚᏔᏟ
ᏝᏴᏬᏟ ᏬᏲᏔᏟ ᏚᏫ ᏝᏞᎤᏬᏟ.

ᏟᏟ ᏞᏟᏐᎤ Ꮪ ᏚᏫ ᏓᏟ ᎿᏆ ᏝᏮᏟᏴᏂ ᏓᏟ ᎿᏆ ᏢᏛᏟ
ᏒᏬ ᏝᏓᏚ ᏓᏃᏙ ᏓᏟ ᏤᏲᎳᏞᎵ Ꭴ ᏴᏟᏗ. Ꮣ4Ꮓ
ᏔᎠᏞᎵ ᏟᏟᏴ ᏟᏟᏘ ᏚᏫ ᏒᎢ ᏟᏞᏝᏴ ᏚᏬᏟᏬᎬ
ᏓᏟ ᏏᏴᏬᏟ ᏟᏟᏴ ᏒᎢ ᏝᏟᏝᏟ ᏳᎡᎠᏬ.
ᏬᏲᏔᏟᏞ ᏓᏔᏚ ᏟᏟᏝᏟ ᏓᏟ ᏟᏞᏝᏴ ᎿᏓᏟᏬᎠ
ᏲᏟ ᏗᏞᏟᏬᎩ ᏚᏫᎤ.

ᏬᎤ ᏬᏞᏗ ᏟᏬᏲᏟᏔ, ᏟᏬᏨ ᏤᏫ ᏟᏲᏮᏢ ᏲᏫ ᎠᏛᏮ ᏝᏬᏟ.

The Oconaluftee River Trail
1.5 miles one-way, or three miles roundtrip; easy

Learn about Cherokee legends and culture along this delightful and easy walking path leading from the Mountain Farm Museum outside the Oconaluftee Visitor Center into the adjoining town of Cherokee.

This is one of two trails you can enjoy with your dog (the other being the Gatlinburg Trail, described previously). Your pet must be on a leash that's six feet or shorter, and you should remember to bring bags to pick up any pet waste. As with the Gatlinburg Trail, you can ride a bike on this trail, and you might be able to use a rugged stroller or wheelchair here, although there are a few small hills in spots.

To avoid backtracking, you can leave a vehicle at one end and make this a 1.5-mile one-way jaunt. Although you'll see signs for a park shuttle near where the trail ends in Cherokee, this is not a shuttle back to the visitor center but is instead a commercial tour operator that takes guests into the park on a loop drive that does not stop at the Oconaluftee Visitor Center (see the shuttle bus section of the chapter on what families need to know).

You could walk this path in either direction, but this description will start at the **Oconaluftee Visitor Center**, where you'll also find

FUN factivity

Look for the hourglass-shaped stump near the second storyboard along the Oconaluftee River Trail. Beavers made this distinctive shape, and the Park Service then cut the tree down to prevent it from falling. Examine it carefully and see if you can find the beaver's teeth marks.

restrooms and vending machines. To get to the trailhead, walk to the start of the path for the Mountain Farm Museum. The Oconaluftee River Trail peels off to the right, at first taking you through a field around the fence that surrounds the museum gardens and buildings.

Before long, you'll head into the woods and along the Oconaluftee River on a hard-packed dirt and gravel path. Keep your kids out of the woods here—there are lots of poison ivy vines.

The walk features **five fascinating bilingual storyboards** along the way that are both in English and in Cherokee symbols (see the chapter on best bets outside the park). Each storyboard features artwork of a different Cherokee artist, and each tells you about a Cherokee legend or tradition that explains the Cherokee's spiritual relationship to that specific place.

The first storyboard shares the legend of a medicine person who fought a great poisonous serpent to get a magical crystal embedded in the great snake's forehead. The next one tells about the tradition of "going to the water" for ritual cleansing.

You'll next walk under an overpass for the Blue Ridge Parkway before coming to the third storyboard. This one tells the tale of the Long Man, who is indeed the river itself, with his head in the mountains and his feet in the sea.

The fourth storyboard shares the Cherokee legend explaining why evergreens are, in fact, ever green and how plants can be used as medicine. After walking over another bridge, you'll come to the last storyboard, which tells the legend of how the Smokies were created, thanks to the wings of a great buzzard forming the mountains and valleys as they brushed against the soft ground.

Near its end, the trail crosses a cutoff road (leading from Newfound Gap Road in the park to Big Cove Road), and then leads up out of the woods to a small grassy spot across from a shopping area on the **Cherokee reservation** (officially called the Qualla Boundary). If you are returning to the visitor center, it's a much safer (and a nicer) walk to double back the way you came rather than returning along busy Newfound Gap Road (U.S. 441).

The six spinster sisters who lived in the Walker sisters' cabin were named Margaret, Polly, Martha, Louisa, Nancy, and Hettie. (One additional sister named Sarah and four brothers also grew up here, but they all married and moved away.) Nancy died before the creation of the national park, but the other five were among those who chose to stay as lifetime lessees. The Walker sisters were known for selling homemade jams, pickles, and crafts to tourists and became somewhat famous after the Saturday Evening Post profiled them on April 27, 1946. The last sister, Louisa, died in 1964 at age 84.

Metcalf Bottoms Trail & Little Brier Gap Trail
3.4 miles roundtrip—maximum; easy

Here's a history hike that combines the **Little Greenbrier Schoolhouse** and the historic **Walker sisters' cabin** (one of the last to be occupied in the park). You can do this hike several different ways, with options to hike 1.2, 2.2, or 3.4 miles roundtrip.

The route begins at the Metcalf Bottoms Picnic Area (see the

Students of Little Greenbrier School, circa 1936 (top), and the school in 1920 (bottom).

chapter on picnicking) off of Little River Road. The hike from there to the schoolhouse (and an adjacent cemetery) is 0.6 mile one-way (1.2 miles roundtrip). To continue the hike to the Walker sisters' cabin, you can take the Little Brier Gap Trail, which goes an additional 1.1 miles from the schoolhouse to the cabin, for a total of 3.4 miles roundtrip.

For a quicker way to see both historic sites if you are pressed for time (or have very small or very tired children), drive over the one-lane bridge at the picnic area and take Wear Cove Gap Road for about a quarter mile until turning right onto a narrow gravel road (closed in winter) that leads to the schoolhouse in half a mile. Park there and hike the 2.2-mile roundtrip segment to the Walker sisters' cabin.

FUN fact

Some students of the Little Greenbrier Schoolhouse walked as far as nine miles to get to school.

In addition to the restrooms near the trailhead at the Metcalf Bottoms Picnic Area, you will also find port-a-johns at the schoolhouse on a seasonal basis.

To start the hike from Metcalf Bottoms, look for the one lane wooden bridge crossing the river in the center of the picnic area. The trailhead is on the far side of the bridge, immediately to the right. This is a wide, fairly flat trail that winds through the woods and past a water tower, taking you over a few small foot bridges and then depositing you at a spot behind the one-room, split-log schoolhouse.

Built from four-foot-wide tuliptree logs in 1882 (by the parents of the schoolchildren themselves), this building also doubled as a Primitive Baptist church on Sundays—hence the adjacent cemetery, surrounded by a picket fence. The schoolhouse was used until 1935—more than 50 years. Inside, you'll see many well-worn wooden desks and a painted-wood blackboard.

To continue to the Walker sisters' cabin, walk up the hill behind the parking area and cemetery (the final resting place for many Walkers and Stinnets) to a gated road leading further uphill. (Although this gravel road is officially called the Little Brier Gap Trail, it isn't labeled as such; instead, there's a sign here indicating that the Walker sisters' cabin is in 1.1 miles.)

The Walker sisters' cabin has two rooms, each with its own stone fireplace. (These were actually two cabins, constructed at different times and later moved together when the sisters were children.) You can poke about the main cabin (be sure to see the remnants of the newspaper that once lined the walls), and view some rusted implements sitting on a shelf. You'll also see some outbuildings here, including a springhouse and a corncrib with tools still hanging on the side. Although these are the only outbuildings you will see now, at one time this was a 122.8-acre farm that also included a barn, a pigpen, a smokehouse, an apple house, a blacksmith shop, and a gristmill.

Old Cadillac Hike (Middle Prong Trail)
Four miles, round trip; easy to moderate

This hike covers the first part of what is officially called the **Middle Prong Trail**, which follows a wide, graded railroad bed left over

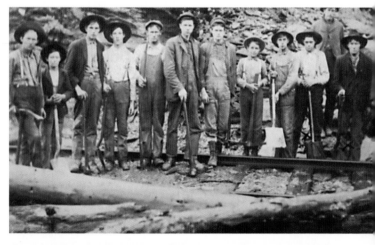

A track-laying crew for the Little River Lumber Company in 1906. It was common for young boys to work in the lumber camps prior to 1938, when the Fair Labor Standards Act was passed by Congress.

from logging days. The entire trail is 4.1 miles one-way, but to see the old, rusting shell of a Cadillac left here from the 1930s, you need only hike two miles in. This is a great hike in the spring when the wildflowers bloom and the waterfalls are robust.

To get to the trailhead, drive the entire 5.2 miles of the Tremont Road (from Laurel Creek Road, just beyond the Townsend "Y". The first two miles of this road are paved, up to a point near the turnoff to the Great Smoky Mountains Institute at Tremont.

The last 3.2-mile segment is a gravel road, which becomes the **Tremont Logging History Auto Tour**. (Follow the guide booklet for this auto tour to learn more about the area's logging history. The booklet is available at visitor centers or from a box near the start of the drive.)

At the end of the gravel road, park your car and walk over the large metal bridge. The area around the bridge used to be the boom town of Tremont—one of three company towns built by the Little River Lumber Company. At one time, this area boasted a post office, a general store, a 22-room hotel, and a community center (that was used as a school during the week and a church and movie theater on the weekends), as well as some maintenance buildings.

Logging continued here until 1939, five years after the park was established (because of agreements the government made with the Little River Lumber Company to acquire the land). That makes this area the last of the parkland to be logged.

The trail starts out following an exceptionally picturesque creek called **Lynn Camp Prong**. You'll pass several cascades and small waterfalls along the way. After 0.7 mile, you'll see a waterfall that appears to be in three rather perfect-looking steps, the remains of a previous logging operation's splash dam (which assisted them in getting the big logs out before the railroads were built), now more than a century old.

After two miles, look for a narrow but very well-worn side trail on the right. It's easy to miss, especially in the fall when leaves cover the path, so look carefully. Here are a few landmarks to help you find it: First, right by the side trail, you'll find a rhododendron bush growing over a rock, its roots wrapping around the large stone. Next to the bush is a smallish-sized forked tree, with a rock about the size of a person's head inexplicably wedged down between its two trunks. (You'll know you've missed the side trail if you come to the junction with the Panther Creek Trail. If that happens, retrace your steps for about a third of a mile.)

Follow this side trail for about 50 yards up and over a berm and then under a very large fallen log to the remains of a rusty old Cadillac. A supervisor of the Civilian Conservation Corps (CCC) camp in this area once owned the car.

The story goes that one day the Caddy quit running, so the men pushed it off the side of the road, where it remains today. Its roof, wheels, and engine are gone, but the frame of the car is still there, along with its doors, part of the hood, its bumpers, and a few springs inside that used to belong to the seats. Of the handful of old cars left rusting in the park, this is probably the most complete. (Be careful to avoid the sharp edges, because some of the metal is jagged.) Turn around here and return to complete the four-mile roundtrip option.

Indian Flats Falls Option: If you're up for a longer hike to a lovely out-of-the-way waterfall (7.5 miles roundtrip, from the start of the Middle Prong Trail; moderate), keep going. At the junction with Panther Creek Trail, continue straight to stay on Middle Prong Trail. About half a mile further, you'll see an old brick chimney marking where a cabin once stood. The remains of the Middle Prong CCC camp (which housed 172 men during the Depression) are also located here.

About a mile farther, right after a wide bridge over Indian Flats Prong, you'll start to go uphill. The trail makes a few rounded turns, and then it makes two sharp switchbacks as it climbs, the first switchback turning to the right and the second to the left. As you approach the second switchback, you'll notice a dark rocky bluff right in front of you. Here, a small side trail leads off to the right for a few hundred feet over rocks and through rhododendron to **Indian Flats Falls**.

When you get there, you'll see the 20-foot falls to the left, dropping into a picturesque little pool. Immediately in front of you is the second drop (you'll be standing level with the lip of the drop), followed a short distance by the falls' third drop, to your right. A fourth drop is well out of sight below you, lost in the tangle of rhododendron. This is a simply magical spot, well worth finding.

(By the way, if you come across the junction with the Greenbrier Ridge Trail and the Miry Ridge Trail, you've gone too far and will need to backtrack. It's actually easier to see the side trail to the falls coming downhill on the main trail than going up.)

Porters Creek Trail
Two miles roundtrip; easy

Although the Porters Creek Trail is actually 3.6 miles in total, the first mile (or the first 1.8 miles, if you want to extend your hike to a waterfall) is the best bet for families. This is a very popular wildflower trail in the spring.

You'll find the trailhead past the Greenbrier Picnic Area at the end of the road from the Greenbrier entrance to the park, off of Route 321 (which runs from Gatlinburg along the northern border of the park).

FUN fact

More than 170 historic cemeteries exist in the park, half of them tiny family plots used for generations in remote locations. Graves most often faced east, the direction from which the Messiah was expected to one day return.

This wide trail follows Porters Creek. Soon after you begin, you'll come across the foundations of various old homesteads, along with their stone walls, steps, a fireplace or two, and even a few springhouse foundations. Poke about the short side trails to see what you can find.

You'll eventually come across steps on the side of the trail that lead to the small **Ownby cemetery**, with 23 graves mostly dating from the early 1900s. Most are simple fieldstones with no inscriptions, while some bear names. You'll also find some modern headstones that descendants erected to replace some of the older, original markers.

Soon after the cemetery, back in the woods on the right side of the

trail, you'll see an axel and a bumper—the remains of an old car. Immediately after this is a half-log bridge, after which the old roadbed ends in a loop. This is **Porters Flat**. You'll find a historic farm site on the right side of the loop road, about 200 yards away. The Porters Creek Trail continues off to the left side of the loop road on a narrower path through the woods.

The historic farm site starts with the **John Messer barn**, a very large renovated cantilevered barn built about 1875. Behind the barn you'll find a springhouse and also a two-room cabin built by the Smoky Mountain Hiking Club in 1934 and used for almost 50 years. The club built the cabin around the original Messer cabin's chimney— all that was left of it at the time. Turn around and backtrack from here, returning to the trailhead.

Fern Branch Falls Option: To extend this hike to a waterfall for a total of 3.6 miles roundtrip, continue on the Porters Creek Trail for just 0.8 mile. After the long footbridge is a fabulous wildflower spot (on the right) and not long after, you'll see 40-foot Fern Branch Falls (on the left).

Flat Creek Trail
2.6 miles one-way, or 5.2 miles roundtrip; moderate
Access road closed to cars in winter

This trail begins high up on **Balsam Mountain**, close to an overlook with a fabulous view. The trail is sometimes referred to by its old name, Flat Creek Falls Trail, although the side trail to the falls is no longer maintained because it is steep, slippery, and very dangerous. If you keep to the main trail, however, a grand high-elevation hike (resplendent with wildflowers in spring and summer) is in store for you.

To get to the trailhead, turn onto Heintooga Ridge Road (closed in winter) at the Balsam Mountain sign from the Blue Ridge Parkway, about 11 miles from where the parkway begins just south of the Oconaluftee Visitor Center. Continue on Heintooga Ridge Road 8.5 miles to its end at the Heintooga Picnic Area and Overlook (closed in

Two Appalachian Trail shelters: Derrick Knob Shelter (top) and Mollies Ridge Shelter. A.T. shelters typically accommodate from 12 to 14 hikers at a time.

winter; see the chapter on picnicking). From the parking area (where you'll also find restrooms), you will see a sign pointing toward the Flat Creek Trail by a roadbed that leads behind the hill where the picnic area begins.

The roadbed goes a short way to a truly fabulous overlook. Not far away, you'll see the Flat Creek Trail leading off to the right of the roadbed. Blackberry bushes grow all along the roadbed by the overlook, offering a sweet snack in August and September. They continue along the trail, as well. If you look, you'll also find a few blueberry bushes.

The trail is fairly easy, with several stream crossings over Flat Creek, although it does get steep for a short portion at the end. If you want to avoid the steep part, turn around when you get to the huge hollow tree on the stream bank, right before one of the half-log bridges.

The trail eventually ends at a point that you passed as you drove in on Heintooga Ridge Road, about 5.3 miles from the road's start on the Blue Ridge Parkway. There isn't a parking lot here, but if you have two cars, you could leave one car parked on the wide area by the side of the road on your drive up and just hike the trail one-way (a 2.6-mile trip). Otherwise, you'll have to double back to return to the picnic area.

An estimated five million steps are required to walk the entire 2,175 miles of the Appalachian Trail. About 2,500 hikers set out to complete the trail each year, but only about 15 to 20 percent of them make it the whole way.

Appalachian Trail
From Newfound Gap to Road Prong Trail
1.7 miles one-way, or 3.4 miles roundtrip; moderate

Perhaps the best-known hiking trail in the U.S. is the Appalachian Trail (affectionately referred to as the A.T.), which travels 2,175 miles through 14 states between Maine and Georgia. For 71.4 of those miles, the A.T. winds through the Smokies, mostly on the Tennessee-North Carolina state line. It crosses Newfound Gap Road (U.S. 441) at Newfound Gap and also leads very close to Clingmans Dome. In fact, the dome is the highest point on the whole A.T.

Although your family may not be up for the entire 2,000-plus-mile trek, it's certainly easy to noodle around on the A.T. for a bit from the parking lot at Newfound Gap (where, by the way, you'll find restrooms). The busier section of the trail from here goes northeast, toward Charlies Bunion (and eventually Maine), so a less crowded option for families is to hike southwest (toward Georgia) along a ridgeline to a place called Indian Gap (where the Road Prong Trail begins). This is especially lovely in fall, when the leaves change colors.

If you have two cars and can hike this one-way, you'll have a more downhill hike if you start at Indian Gap and hike to Newfound Gap. But this is not an option in winter, when Clingmans Dome Road is closed.

The Appalachian Trail is marked by a distinctive white blaze—a white rectangle, usually painted on the trees by the side of the trail. See how many of these blazes you can find along this stretch of the trail.

To start from Newfound Gap, cross U.S. 441 at the crosswalk and turn left to find the trailhead. You'll not only be following the A.T., you'll also be walking on the state line between Tennessee and North Carolina for the whole hike.

FUN fact

Earl Shaffer, a longtime resident of Idaville, Pennsylvania, was the first person to walk the entire Appalachian Trail, which he accomplished in 1948 at the age of 29. In 1965, he did the same thing in the opposite direction, becoming the first person to hike the entire trail both ways. In 1998, the 50th anniversary of his first trek, he made the trip a third and final time before his death in 2002. The log cabin he lived in (located just five miles from the A.T.) had electricity for only the last two years of Shaffer's life. It never had running water.

After the second downhill portion is a special kind of fence designed to protect an area of beech forest from the park's destructive wild hogs. You'll walk up a grated incline here that the hogs cannot negotiate with their small hooves. These non-native animals are descendants of European wild boars that escaped from a hunting preserve in North Carolina in the 1920s and mated with domestic pigs from local farms. Every night, these nocturnal beasts root around in search of food, destroying the delicate vegetation of the forest floor and threatening many species.

This enclosure, built in 1984, is one of 20 such fenced-in sites in the park that protect high-elevation beech forest communities, which are unique to the southern Appalachians. In about 150 yards, you'll go through an identical fence to leave the enclosed area.

The trail ends where you walk out of the woods to a pull-off on Clingmans Dome Road at a place called Indian Gap, 1.4 miles from Newfound Gap. You'll be at 5,272 feet in elevation here, just eight feet short of a mile high.

SMOKIES PARK TALLY

Keep a running count during your trip of some of the different things you notice each day as you explore the park. Make a tally mark next to the appropriate category below for each thing you see. If you want, you can change to a different category each day of your visit, or you can use multiple categories each day. See if you can come up with a few your own categories, too.

Birds ◯	Deer ◯	Bears ◯
Salamanders ◯	Butterflies ◯	Park rangers ◯
Log buildings ◯	Historic churces ◯	Bridges ◯
Waterfalls ◯	Nature trails ◯	Roadside displays ◯

CHAPTER 13

Camping

Sleeping in the Smokies pretty much means camping. You won't find any other overnight accommodation in the park—unless you're one of the hardy souls hiking to Le Conte Lodge on the summit of Mount Le Conte (see the chapter on hikes with a view) or unless you're signed up for a residential program at the Great Smoky Mountains Institute at Tremont (see the chapter on ranger programs and educational opportunities).

Whether you wake up to birdsong in the morning or sit around a crackling campfire watching for shooting stars in the inky night sky, the Smokies can give your kids an up-close-and-personal experience with nature that they just won't get at a resort or hotel.

To that end, the park offers more than 1,100 sites in ten developed campgrounds (referred to as frontcountry campgrounds) plus about one hundred backcountry sites for hard-core backpackers who prefer being even further off the grid. Generally, two campgrounds stay open year-round—Cades Cove in Tennessee and Smokemont in North Carolina. The others are open from the spring through the fall. (Exact dates of operation vary with the individual campground and also from year to year, so call the park or check the park's website for more specific information.)

Campgrounds in the park range from intimate places with only 12 sites tucked away in the woods to relatively massive 200-site communities teeming with kids of all ages. Each has its own appeal. Larger campgrounds may be busier, but they're also more likely to have ranger programs and activities.

The Smokies also has five drive-in horse camps—primitive campgrounds with anywhere from two to seven sites each that have hitch racks for horses. They're open from spring through fall at Anthony Creek (in Cades Cove), Big Creek, Cataloochee, Round Bottom (near Oconaluftee), and Tow String (also near Oconaluftee). Of the five, only Big Creek has flush toilets with cold water. The others have pit toilets and no drinking water. (The Big Creek horse camp also has one site that is handicapped accessible.)

All but two (Look Rock and Balsam Mountain) are on or near streams. Most accommodate tents (on 13-foot-square tent pads), pop-up trailers, and RVs, and each individual campsite is limited to six people (in either two tents or one RV plus one tent). All but

The crisp nights of autumn make camping in the mountains an especially rich experience.

three campgrounds also offer a limited number of group camping areas that must be reserved in advance. You can bring your pet as long as you keep the animal on a leash or restrain it in some way at all times.

Most individual sites are level, and each has a fire ring with a grate for cooking and a picnic table (usually with a lantern pole). Many have handicapped-accessible facilities.

Each campground has restrooms with cold running water and flush toilets, but no showers. (You can, however, easily get a shower in the gateway communities surrounding the park.) Individual campsites do not have electrical or water hookups. Half the campgrounds have dump stations for RVs, and the Sugarlands Visitor Center also has a dump station in case the campground you pick doesn't.

Camping fees vary with the time of year and the campground but are generally pretty affordable. The maximum stay is seven days during the summer and fall, and 14 days during the off-season.

Half of the park's campgrounds operate on a first-come, first-serve basis. Both the smaller and the more popular campgrounds like Cataloochee, Abrams Creek, Deep Creek, and Big Creek typically fill up on weekends, so if you want to stay there, either come during the week to score your spot or arrive early on Friday.

Five campgrounds (Elkmont, Smokemont, Cades Cove, Cataloochee, and Cosby) do accept reservations, but only for stays from May 15 through October 31. Usually, reserving only a few weeks out is sufficient, although you can make reservations up to six months in advance—a good idea if you're coming on a holiday weekend. To make reservations, either visit www.recreation.gov or call 1-877-444-6777 from 10 a.m. to

10 p.m. Reservations are required at Cataloochee's small campground.

Everyone who comes to the Smokies wants to see bears, but you definitely *don't* want to see them in your campsite! Take bear-proofing suggestions seriously and follow campground regulations to avoid problems and stay safe. For example, keep all food and food preparation equipment (stoves, pots, coolers, etc.) in your car or a solid-sided camper. Balsam Mountain, Big Creek, Cades Cove, Cataloochee, Cosby, Deep Creek, Elkmont, and Smokemont all have food storage lockers for the few campers who need them (like motorcyclists). Don't leave any garbage or food wrappers lying around—use the dumpsters. If you leave a cooler out, the rangers will probably impound it (and slap you with a fine) if the bears don't get it first!

Please note: Don't bring firewood from home when you come to the Smokies. The U.S. Department of Agriculture has quarantined firewood from most eastern and midwestern states to prevent the spread of two small but highly destructive insects that may be living in the wood. One is a metallic green bug called the emerald ash borer and the other is the black and white Asian longhorned beetle. Both could potentially destroy the forests in the park if the Smokies became infested.

Once you arrive, you can buy firewood in a handful of the campgrounds or in the communities surrounding the park. (You're also permitted to collect dead wood that's on the ground.) If you brought wood from quarantined states with you without knowing about the ban, the best thing to do is to burn it as soon as possible.

What follows are brief descriptions of each campground. Please see the appropriate chapters on picnicking and on self-guiding nature trails for details about the specific examples of those mentioned below.

Elkmont
closed in winter

Popular and busy Elkmont is the largest of all the park's campgrounds, with 220 sites—including two that are handicapped accessible. The most popular sites here are on the water—mostly along the **Little River**, although a handful are along the smaller **Jakes Creek**.

Elkmont Campground has a **self-guiding nature trail** (0.8 mile roundtrip), an **amphitheater** where a large number of ranger programs are held, **pay phone service**, and a **concession area** that sells wood and ice. Recently, the concession items have expanded to include a small assortment of convenience items, such as camp fuel, toiletries and drug store items, tent stakes, and even some food items—including the all-important makings for s'mores (chocolate bars, marshmallows, and graham crackers). The concession stand can also charge camera batteries and blow up inflatables. This area also has vending machines for drinks and snacks.

FUN fact

Elkmont Campground sits on land that was originally a farm. From 1908 until 1926, this area was a logging town owned by the Little River Lumber Company. A company store, post office, church, school, hotel, and railroad all operated where people now pitch tents and toast marshmallows.

To get to Elkmont, turn at the Elkmont sign on Little River Road (between Metcalf Bottoms Picnic Area and Sugarlands Visitor Center), and then drive 1.5 miles to the campground.

Cosby
closed in winter

Cosby Campground's wooded setting is idyllic. It's a favorite of many campers because it is off the beaten path (although only about a half hour's drive from the Sugarlands Visitor Center), it offers plenty of sites to choose from (165 in all—including two that are handicapped accessible), and it rarely fills up. There's also a dump station here for RVs.

The **Cosby Picnic Area** is right before the entrance to the campground, and the enchanting **Cosby Self-Guiding Nature Trail** (one mile roundtrip) starts directly across from the campground's amphitheater, where special ranger programs are occasionally offered. The trailhead for the **Gabes Mountain Trail**, which leads to **Hen Wallow Falls** (4.4 miles roundtrip) is immediately before the picnic area and not far from the campground entrance, although there's an additional side trail from section A of the campground, as well.

To get to the campground, turn into the park at the Cosby entrance off of Route 32 along the northern boundary of the park. The campground is about a two-mile drive from the entrance.

Cades Cove

Cades Cove's 159 campsites (including five that are handicapped accessible) are among the most popular in the park, even though the campground is more crowded than most. One reason for its popularity is that it sits just outside the 11-mile **Cades Cove Loop Road** (see the chapter on scenic drives).

But that's not all this busy campground has to offer. This is the only campground in the park that has a **full camp store** (open from mid-March through early November; 1-865-448-9034) selling all sorts of groceries, camping supplies, convenience items, firewood, and ice. The camp store houses a snack bar selling breakfast items, hot and cold sandwiches and wraps, soup and chili, pizza, soft serve ice cream, fountain drinks, and other food items. The store even takes credit cards.

You'll also find a new **gift shop** and a **bike rental shop** (see the chapter on biking) located next to the **amphitheater**, where many ranger programs and special events take place. What's more, the trailhead for the **Cades Cove Nature Trail** (0.5 mile roundtrip) is in section C of the campground, as is a **dump station** for RVs. This campground also has **pay phone service** and **vending machines**.

On the way into the campground, you'll pass a turnoff for the **Cades Cove Picnic Area,** and then you will pass the **Cades Cove Riding Stables** (closed in winter) before you get to the campground. The stables offer carriage rides and hayrides, in addition to horseback riding. In high season, some of the hayrides are ranger-guided.

You'll find the entrance to the campground off of Laurel Creek Road just before the start of the 11-mile Cades Cove Loop Road.

One of the spectacular views in Cades Cove, seen from Rich Mountain Road.

Smokemont

Smokemont Campground in North Carolina is one of the larger of the park's campgrounds, with 142 sites—including two that are handicapped accessible—many of them right on the river. Opened in 1938, this is also the oldest campground in the park (although it's been upgraded as the years have gone by). During the peak season, this popular campground offers some ranger programs based at the **amphitheater**.

A 0.75-mile loop trail begins near site #31 in section B. Just outside the entrance to the campground (to the right after you cross the bridge on the way in) is the **Smokemont Riding Stables** (closed in winter). The stables also sell **firewood** and **ice**. (There are **vending machines** here, too.) Just past the stables is a **dump station** for RVs.

In-between the stables and the campground, you'll also find the historic **Smokemont Baptist Church**, a restored clapboard building dating from 1912. To get there, look for the small gravel parking lot immediately across from the bridge that you crossed on the way in.

Smokemont Campground is situated on the banks of the Oconaluftee River.

From this gravel lot, you'll find a short path leading up the hill to the church (although the leaves often hide this building from the main road during the summer).

The Smokemont Campground is on Newfound Gap Road (U.S. 441), two miles from the **Collins Creek Picnic Area**, three miles from **Mingus Mill**, and just over three miles from the **Oconaluftee Visitor Center** and the **Mountain Farm Museum**. It's not much farther from the town of **Cherokee** in the Qualla Boundary (the name for the Cherokee reservation).

> ### FUN fact
>
> *Take your kids into the Smokemont Campground office to show them the display of photographs of the historic Smokemont logging camp, including the 1920 sawmill complex that once stood where the campground is now. This was one of 15 large sawmills that existed in the early 1900s in what is now the national park.*

Deep Creek
closed in winter

Deep Creek Campground's 92 sites—including one that is handicapped accessible—are basically divided into two sections. A mass of **tent sites** sits all together on a fairly treeless river bank, while a group of more private **wooded sites** are just a bit uphill to the right. Deep Creek has a **dump station** for RVs.

The **Deep Creek Picnic Area** is just beyond the entrance to the campground, and the **Three Waterfalls Loop hike** (2.4 miles roundtrip) begins just down the road from the picnic area.

Deep Creek is at the southern edge of the park, near Bryson City. To get to the campground from town, follow the signs leading into the park, and then at the sign for the campground entrance, make a right-hand turn, crossing a small bridge over Deep Creek.

Look Rock
closed in winter

Look Rock Campground, with its 68 wooded sites, is located high on a ridgeline on the western edge of the park. Because it's somewhat out of the way, it doesn't get a lot of traffic. It's quiet and peaceful here, and it almost never fills up—even on summer holiday weekends.

This campground (the park's highest on the Tennessee side) has an **amphitheater** for special programs and a **dump station** for RVs. It's also next to the **Look Rock Picnic Area**, and a walking trail leads from here to the **Look Rock Tower Trail**.

To get there, take the Foothills Parkway West (see the chapter on scenic drives) from Townsend, and turn left at the sign for the campground at about the midpoint.

Balsam Mountain
closed in winter

Sitting on its lofty perch at 5,310 feet—more than a mile high—the Balsam Mountain Campground is the highest elevation campground in the park. Because of the elevation, nights are cool here even in the middle of the summer, and daytime highs are relatively mild.

This campground is small and many of its 46 sites are fairly together—but because it's fairly remote, it's also one of the less crowded campgrounds. Ranger programs occasionally take place in the campground's **amphitheater**.

The trailhead for the **Balsam Mountain Self-Guiding Nature Trail** (one mile roundtrip) is just inside the entrance, next to site #44. The **Heintooga Picnic Area and Overlook** are just a half mile further down the road, as is the trailhead for the **Flat Creek Trail** (5.2 miles roundtrip).

To get there from the Oconaluftee Visitor Center, take the Blue Ridge Parkway to milepost 458 and turn left at the big sign for Balsam Mountain onto Heintooga Ridge Road (closed in winter). The campground is eight miles from the turn.

FUN fact

Most campgrounds in the park have one or more resident campground hosts, volunteers who camp in the park for weeks at a time, assisting the rangers, helping to keep the campground clean, and answering questions from visitors. In exchange for their service, the park supplies them with a free camping spot.

Cataloochee
closed in winter

Since the elk reintroduction program began in 2001 (see the chapter on animals), the fairly small and remote Cataloochee Campground has become much more popular, often filling up on weekends. Consequently, reservations are now required to camp at Cataloochee. A creek flows past many of the campground's 27 sites, which are right down the road from the start of the Cataloochee Auto Tour (see the chapter on scenic drives).

To get there from I-40, take exit #20 in North Carolina and turn right onto Cove Creek Road, following the signs 11 miles into the Cataloochee Valley. To get there from Oconaluftee or Cherokee, take the Blue Ridge Parkway to Highway 19. Follow this road through Maggie Valley and turn left onto Highway 276 N. Just before the entrance ramp to I-40, turn left and follow the signs 11 miles to Cataloochee.

With either route, the last three of these 11 miles are down a well-maintained gravel road. When you see the paved road, turn left. This will lead to the campground, which will be on your left.

Abrams Creek
closed in winter

Abrams Creek may not be the smallest campground in the park, but with only 16 sites, it runs a pretty close second. (And it *is* the smallest campground where you can take an RV.) A little over half of the sites in this jewel are right on Abrams Creek. Although this is a remote campground on the western edge of the park, it often fills up quickly on weekends because of its size and popularity with locals. Abrams Creek is a relatively short drive from the Foothills Parkway West (see the chapter on scenic drives), as well as from the Look Rock Campground and picnic area and the Look Rock Tower Trail (one mile roundtrip).

Getting to this campground is a bit of a trip. To find it, drive southwest on the Foothills Parkway from Townsend, and take the turnoff toward the Look Rock Campground, at about the halfway point of the parkway. But immediately after taking the turnoff, before the picnic area or the Look Rock Campground entrance, take a sharp right-hand turn downhill onto the unmarked Butterfly Gap Road. Drive a short while before taking the next right turn, a sharp turn onto Flats Road that continues going downhill for a longer distance. Take the first left-hand turn, onto Happy Valley Road, which is so sharp it's practically a U-turn. Stay on this road for some time as it winds through the countryside outside the park. At the sign for the Abrams Creek Campground, turn left onto the unmarked Abrams Creek Road, which proceeds into the park. You'll pass the ranger station and begin following the creek before arriving at the campground at the end of the road.

For an alternate route that's near the intersection of the Foothills Parkway West and Highway 129, turn on to Happy Valley Road and follow it all the way to Abrams Creek Campground.

Big Creek
closed in winter

Big Creek is the park's smallest campground (with only 12 sites), and it's also the only campground in the park that doesn't allow RVs—it's for **tents only**. The spacious sites overlook Big Creek, and they're set way back from the road, tucked into the woods in a truly intimate setting. Carts are available to help campers tote their gear the requisite 100 to 300 feet from their cars to their tent sites.

Because of its size (not to mention its unique nature), Big Creek tends to fill up quickly on weekends. The lovely **Big Creek Picnic Area** is near the entrance to the campground, just past the horse camp and the group camping area.

The Big Creek Trail in autumn.

Big Creek is located near the Tennessee-North Carolina state line. To get there from I-40, take Tennessee exit #451 and follow the road for two miles (only paved for the first mile) to the park's Big Creek entrance. An alternate route on the Tennessee side is to turn onto Route 32 in Cosby and follow this very winding, slow road (paved except for the last mile) to Big Creek. This route is not recommended for those who are easily carsick.

Big Creek Campground is located on the site of an old logging town named Crestmont.

CHAPTER 14

Biking

You won't find any true mountain biking trails in the national park, although biking is permitted on all the park's roads. Even so, most of them are too steep, too narrow, too winding, and too busy for safe and fun family biking.

Stick to the places mentioned below (or bike around the campgrounds) for the best Smoky Mountain cycling experience.

Cades Cove

Hands-down, the best place for biking in the park is the 11-mile **Cades Cove Loop Road** (see the chapter on scenic drives)—on Wednesday and Saturday mornings in the summer, when the road is closed to automobile traffic until 10:00 a.m. This pedal-friendly policy starts the second week in May and continues through the second-to-last Saturday in September.

You'll enjoy a very peaceful ride during this time, a totally different experience than riding through the exhaust of the cars that snake their way around the loop later in the day. Morning is also prime time to see wildlife, so look out for critters (especially deer). You can also visit some of the historic sites along the way (and return later in your car to see the rest).

While much of the loop road is fairly flat, the far side of the cove includes some very steep grades and a few sharp blind curves. However, if you cut across Cades Cove on either of the two roads through the middle, you can avoid all of these challenges and still have a great bike ride. Taking the **Sparks Lane** cut-off makes for a four-mile loop ride, and if you take the **Hyatt Lane** cut-off a little further down the road, your ride will be a total of eight miles.

If you haven't brought your own bikes with you, you can rent them from the **Cades Cove bike rental shop** (1-865-448-9034; www.explorecadescove.com) in the Cades Cove Campground (see the chapter

FUN *fact*

Cades Cove covers 6,800 acres. That's more than eight times the size of New York City's Central Park or more than six times the space that Magic Kingdom, Epcot, Disney's Hollywood Studios, and Animal Kingdom take up together).

on camping), near the start of the loop drive. The bike shop is open from mid-March through early November, seven days a week, from 9:00 a.m. to 4:30 p.m. (in summer) or until 2:30 p.m. (in spring and fall). (The bike shop opens at 7:00 a.m. on those mornings that the loop drive is closed to cars.) All bikes must be back by 8 p.m.

Bikes are rented by the hour on a first-come, first-serve basis, and they go quickly in the summer (particularly in July and early August), so plan to start as close to the 7:00 a.m. opening time as possible.

Rental bikes are new each season, so they're in great shape. Most are geared bikes (with 27 gears). You can also rent a few cruisers (bikes without gears that require you to pedal backward to brake) for about $2 per hour less. Smaller children's bikes (both with and without gears) are also available at a lower rate. Helmets are free to all renters—in fact, Tennessee law requires children age 16 and under to wear them.

The rental shop requires all bike riders to wear closed-toe shoes (no sandals), and you must leave either a $50 deposit or your car keys at the time of the rental.

Beyond Cades Cove

A few other areas in the park are also bike-friendly. Four hiking/walking trails (three of them in North Carolina) allow bikes. Two of them are the **Gatlinburg Trail** from the Sugarlands Visitor Center to Gatlinburg (two miles one-way; four miles roundtrip) and the **Oconaluftee River Trail** from the Oconaluftee Visitor Center to Cherokee (1.5 miles one-way, or three miles roundtrip).

The other two bikable trails are the lower graveled sections of both the **Deep Creek** and the **Indian Creek** trails in the Deep Creek section of the park, near Bryson City, NC. On the Deep Creek Trail, you can bike on a two-mile stretch from the trailhead near Deep Creek Campground to the end of the graveled surface. On the Indian Creek Trail, you can bike on an additional 2.9-mile segment from where the trail begins (at the junction with the Deep Creek Trail) to the junction with the Deeplow Gap Trail.

For a great double-waterfall biking tour, start at the trailhead for the Deep Creek Trail and bike 0.2 mile to Tom Branch Falls (see the chapter on waterfall hikes), which you'll see on the right. Continue riding a half mile more, and then turn right onto Indian Creek Trail. Just 200 feet after this junction, on the left side of the trail, get off your bikes and walk down the bank to see Indian Creek Falls. Back on your bikes, continue up this trail for 2.9 miles before the gravel ends and you have to turn around. If you bike this whole way, it makes for a 7.2-mile ride roundtrip.

To add the area's third waterfall to your explorations, either before or after your bike trip, hike the short **Juney Whank Falls Trail** (0.6 mile roundtrip), which also starts at the beginning of the Deep Creek Trail. (You won't be able to ride your bikes on this trail, though.)

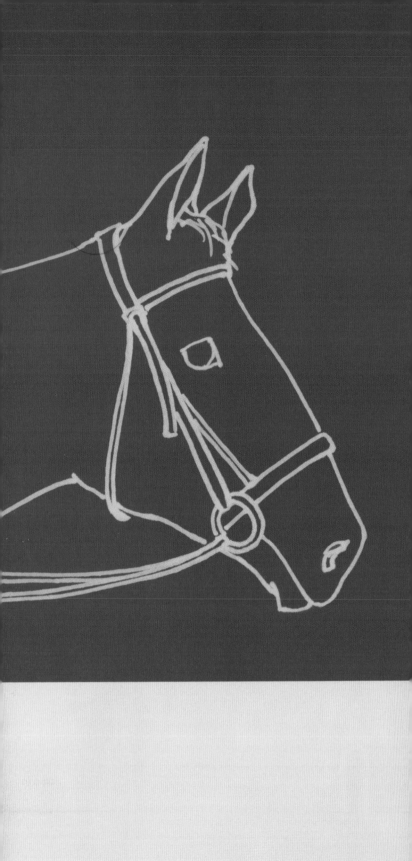

CHAPTER 15

Horseback Riding, Hayrides, Carriage Rides, & Wagon Rides

Seeing the park from horseback can get your family further back into the park (and even higher up) easier and faster than you could hike on your own—not to mention the fact that it's also a ton of fun (or at least a half a ton, literally).

The four different places where it pays to horse around in the park include Cades Cove Riding Stables, Smoky Mountain Riding Stables, and Sugarland Riding Stables in Tennessee and Smokemont Riding Stables in North Carolina. All offer a variety of guided trips (the shortest is one hour) that are suitable for beginners as well as more experienced riders. The horses are gentle, the pace is slow, and the experienced wrangler-guides give instruction and plenty of help when needed. Two of the stables (Smokemont and Cades Cove) also offer hayrides, carriage rides, and/or wagon rides.

The stables are generally open from 9 a.m. to about 5 p.m. daily from mid-March through late November (although exact hours and closing dates vary, so please call ahead). Rates generally range from $20 to $25 per hour, but are subject to change. Each stable has a weight limit (between 225 and 250 lbs), and riders need to be at least five years old. Each rider must be on his or her own horse—there's no doubling up, even with children. Expect to sign a waiver before you ride, as well.

Ask your guide what the names of each of the horses are in your group, and then try to memorize the names by the time your ride is over.

Except for special group rides arranged in advance, the stables don't take reservations for horseback riding. They operate strictly on a first-come, first-serve basis. However, reservations are recommended for the carriage rides, wagon rides, and hayrides (except for the ranger-led hayrides, which are first-come, first-serve).

All the stables in the park have restrooms and vending machines for drinks (and some also have vending machines with snacks). In addition, all of them can accommodate high-functioning disabled guests for horseback riding, although only the restrooms at Smokemont and Sugarlands riding stables are handicapped accessible.

Here's a rundown on your options.

Cades Cove Riding Stables
Closed in winter

Cades Cove Riding Stables (1-865-448-9009) are located near the beginning of the Cades Cove Loop Road (see the chapter on scenic drives). The wrangler-guides here will take you through the woods, over mountain streams, and up gentle mountainsides for lovely views.

In addition to trail rides, Cades Cove also offers narrated 1.5-hour **hayrides** (handicapped accessible), new narrated half-hour **wagon rides** (for four to six passengers; handicapped accessible), and narrated half-hour **horse-drawn carriage rides** around Cades Cove. Although horseback riding doesn't require reservations, the hayrides, wagon rides, and carriage rides do, with one exception—the evening and early-morning hayrides led by park rangers are first-come, first-serve. The charge for the ranger-led hayrides is slightly more than for the regular hayrides. Check the park newspaper for exact dates and times of these trips, which are usually the best for seeing wildlife.

Cades Cove Riding Stables also offer souvenir photographs as well as a limited selection of t-shirts, hats, patches, and similar souvenir items.

To get to the stables, take Laurel Creek Road (which begins at the Townsend entrance to the park, where Little River Road ends). Drive to the end of the road toward Cades Cove and take the turnoff on the left toward the campground before the loop drive begins. Bear right after the turnoff.

Smokemont Riding Stables
Closed in winter

Smokemont Riding Stables (1-828-497-2373; www.smokemontridingstable.com) are located near the Smokemont Campground (see the chapter on camping). The rides include wooded trails, a tunnel under Newfound Gap Road, an easy crossing over the Oconaluftee River, and mountain vistas. One of the most popular offerings is a 2.5-hour ride to **Chasteen Creek Falls**, a gently sloping cascade that rushes and tumbles over the rocks for about 50 feet.

Smokemont also offers half-hour **horse-drawn wagon rides** for four to six passengers on the historic Oconaluftee Turnpike, one of the earliest routes through the mountains. (However, note that unlike at Cades Cove, Smokemont's wagons are *not* handicapped accessible.) Souvenir photos are now available here, too, as well as a limited selection of t-shirts and hats.

The stables are three miles from the Oconaluftee Visitor Center off of Newfound Gap Road (U.S. 441). To get there, turn at the sign for Smokemont Campground. Follow the road over a wooden bridge, and then immediately turn right. (The campground is to the left immediately after the bridge.)

In addition to Smokemont Campground and the Oconaluftee Visitor Center, the Mountain Farm Museum, Mingus Mill, and Collins Creek Picnic Area are all within three miles.

Smoky Mountain Riding Stables
Closed in winter

Smoky Mountain Riding Stables (1-865-436-5634; www.smokymountainridingstables.com) are located just over halfway between Gatlinburg and the Greenbrier entrance to the park. The horseback rides here are fun at any time, but this is a particularly handy option when the wait at the nearby Sugarlands Riding Stables (run by the same outfitter) is too long during peak season.

The trails here wind through the woods and cross pretty mountain streams. Beginners are best served by the shorter rides, while the longer rides on slightly steeper terrain are more appropriate for riders with more experience.

To get to the stables, drive east from downtown Gatlinburg for 4.5 miles on Route 321, which runs along the northern border of the park. The stables will be on the right.

You'll also find the Roaring Fork Motor Nature Trail, the Noah "Bud" Ogle Self-Guiding Nature Trail, the Greenbrier Picnic Area, and the Porters Creek Trail

Sugarlands Riding Stables
Closed in winter

Sugarlands Riding Stables (1-865-436-3535; www.sugarlandsridingstables.com) are located very close to the Sugarlands Visitor Center on Newfound Gap Road (U.S. 441). These stables, run by the same outfitter as the Smoky Mountain Riding Stables just down the road, offer the steepest rides in the park. Even so, beginners will have no trouble on the shorter rides. The most popular option here is the two-hour trip, which shows off three great vistas.

To get there from the Sugarlands Visitor Center, travel 0.6 mile on Newfound Gap Road (U.S. 441) toward Gatlinburg. The stables will be on your right. To get there from Gatlinburg, drive one mile into the park from the Gatlinburg entrance. The stables will be on your left.

In addition to the Sugarlands Visitor Center, you'll find the Fighting Creek Self-Guiding Nature Trail, the Cataract Falls Trail, the Gatlinburg Trail, and the Sugarlands Valley Self-Guiding Nature Trail all within about a mile of the stables (but not open to horses).

Riding your own horse

You can ride a horse on 550 of the park's 800 miles of hiking trails, so if you have a horse, you'll be able to cover a lot of terrain in the park. Please note that you must stick to the trails specified for horses, however. Off-trail riding isn't permitted.

To determine which trails you can take, get one of the park's official trail maps, which also explains the park's rules about horseback riding in the backcountry. (This map is a more detailed one than the free map distributed at the visitor centers.) You can buy trail maps for about a $1 at any of the visitor centers, or you can order them from the Great Smoky Mountains Association either online (at www.SmokiesInformation.org) or by calling 1-865-436-7318, extension 226.

Camping with your horse

The park also offers five drive-in horse camps—primitive campgrounds with anywhere from two to seven sites each with hitch racks for horses. They're open from spring through fall at Anthony Creek (in Cades Cove), Big Creek, Cataloochee, Round Bottom (near Oconaluftee), and Tow String (also near Oconaluftee). Of the five, only Big Creek has flush toilets with cold water. The others have pit toilets and no drinking water. The Big Creek horse camp also has one site that is handicapped accessible.

SMOKY MOUNTAINS ALPHABET SEARCH

Starting with the letter A, look for something as you hike or drive through the park that begins with each letter of the alphabet. Then fill it in below. The first letter is done for you as an example. (For extra fun, find something else that begins with the letter A and write that down, too!) See how many things you can find.

A corn _____

B _____

C _____

D _____

E _____

F _____

G _____

H _____

I _____

J _____

K _____

L _____

M _____

N _____

O _____

P _____

Q _____

R _____

S _____

T _____

U _____

V _____

W _____

X _____

Y _____

Z _____

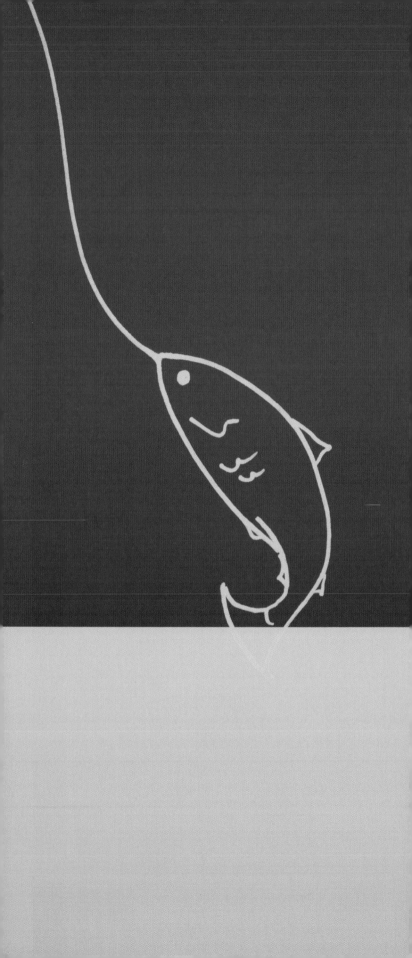

CHAPTER 16

Fishing

The Smokies is a great spot for anglers, with hundreds of miles of fishable water in some 300 streams that contain abundant fish life (two to four thousand trout per mile, in many places). According to park surveys, in the average two- to three-hour fishing trip, most park fishermen hook four to five fish.

Although over 60 species of fish live here, most of the fishing frenzy is around the three species of trout—brook, rainbow, and brown. In fact, the park is one of the last wild trout habitats in the eastern U.S. Of the three species, only the southern Appalachian brook trout (also called brookies or specs by mountain folk) is native to this area. The others were stocked in park streams starting in the early 1900s, after the effects of the logging industry greatly reduced the brook trout population.

Fish live in less than half (38 percent) of the park's 2,115 total miles of rivers and streams.

The rainbows and browns are larger and more aggressive than the native brook trout. In fact, they've more or less muscled the poor brookies out of the way. Today, brook trout live in 182 miles of park streams, mostly above 3,000 feet in elevation—neighborhoods considered undesirable by the rainbows and browns. As a result, their range has shrunk by a whopping 75 percent. (For Americans, that would be like losing all the states west of Lake Michigan.)

Yet the latest news is good: The Park Service's efforts to restore the brook trout to their former habitat have been so successful that since 2006, fisherman have been allowed to fish for brookies in all but three streams in the park for the first time in 30 years.

Fishing regulations

Fishing is permitted year-round in the park, from a half hour before sunrise to a half hour after sunset. You can fish in just about any stream, although some are closed to anglers at various times. For the most updated information about where you can and can't fish, as well as a free map of fishable park waters, ask for a fishing regulations folder at any visitor center or ranger station. You can also check bulletin boards throughout the park for updates.

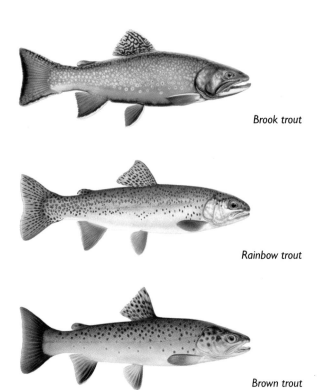

Brook trout

Rainbow trout

Brown trout

Adults will need a **fishing license**. Either a Tennessee or North Carolina state license will do for anywhere that fishing is allowed inside the park boundaries. (No trout stamp is required.) Children 12 and under in Tennessee and 15 and under in North Carolina don't need a license (although the same creel limits and other regulations apply for them as for adults).

The park itself doesn't sell fishing licenses, but you can typically buy them in sporting goods stores and hardware stores in the towns outside the park as well as at the Gatlinburg Welcome Center. For a small premium, you can also buy a license instantly over the phone (by calling 1-888-814-8972) or online (at www.tnwildlife.org or www.ncwildlife.org) using a credit card.

If you want to fish outside the park in Gatlinburg or in Cherokee, by the way, you will need special permits from those locations.

All trout and smallmouth bass must be seven inches or more to keep. You must immediately release anything you catch that's smaller. You can, however, keep any size rock bass you catch. The creel limit is five of any combination of types of fish per day, although you can keep 20 additional rock bass over and above this limit.

You must use artificial flies or lures—no live bait is permitted, nor is using any sort of food (such as corn, bread, cheese, etc.) for bait. In addition, you can only use single hooks.

Moving rocks to build channels and rock dams is illegal. Some fish build their nests in the little spaces underneath the rocks, and these

FUN *fact*

More than 10,000 angler days are logged each year in the park.

nests are destroyed and the hatchlings die when people move the rocks. Also, many aquatic insects actually attach themselves to rocks and cannot move. They can fall, be crushed or dry out and die if people move the rocks they're on.

A Who's Who of park fish

Brook trout are practically the only game fish that live in the headwaters of streams above 3,500 feet in elevation. These are the little guys in the 'hood, with only four percent reaching even seven inches long (although the largest of them can grow to 10 inches). Their bodies have light spots and a worm-like patterns along their backs. They also have distinctive white stripes on their lower fins.

They prefer eddies and calm pockets in cold, clear streams shaded by tall trees. The best spots for them are the higher elevations of Deep Creek, Bradley Fork, and the Middle Prong of the Little River.

Rainbow trout start to appear downstream from the brookies, mixing with them for a while. Rainbows are the most abundant and most commonly caught fish in the park, with most between four and eight inches long. Some fishermen have caught rainbows that were longer than a foot. These fish have light silvery bodies with dark spots, pinkish or reddish bands on their sides, and green backs. They also have spots all over their tailfins.

Rainbows prefer swifter currents and tumbling pocket waters in most park streams. You can also catch them below cascades. Try grey hackles, light cahill, and adams in the spring and royal coachman and other orange-bodied flies in the summer and fall. Other good lures for rainbows include the rooster tail, popping bugs, and spinners. Some of the best fishing for rainbows is in the Little River, Abrams Creek, Hazel Creek, Deep Creek, Oconaluftee River, Bradley Creek, and Cataloochee Creek.

Brown trout start to show up lower still in elevation, sharing space with the rainbows. The browns are the largest of the park's fish, commonly from eight to 20 inches long. A few have even measured 30 inches! These fish have generally brownish-yellow bodies with dark spots on a light background, often with red, orange, or brown spots on their sides. Their tailfins either have no spots or spots just on the top.

Brown trout prefer deep pools and slower waters with plenty of cover to protect them from predators. They also hang out under boulders in pocket waters. Dusk and dawn can be the best times to catch them. The best lures for browns are the same as for rainbow trout, with the addition of streamers. Good streams for browns include the Elkmont area of Little River, Big Creek, and the Oconaluftee River.

Smallmouth and rock (or redeye) bass live at the lowest elevations, near the park boundaries. They're fairly small, but some in Abrams Creek have weighed in at three to five pounds. The smallmouth bass is a bronze color with either a plain side or distinctive vertical stripes on the upper half of its side. The rock bass is less slender and olive to brassy green in color with dark mottling. It sports a large lower fin with six spines and 10 or 11 rays fanning out along a large stretch of its body.

Bass prefer deep pools or shaded areas along the bank. For these fish, use dry and wet flies, popping bugs, and any of a variety of spinners. For the best bass fishing, try Abrams Creek below Abrams Falls, Little River's lower section (near Townsend), and the coves and point of Fontana Lake.

Best fishing streams

FUN fact

Many fisherman claim Abrams Creek is the best trout fishing in the park, and now there's scientific evidence explaining why. This is the one spot in the park where the water flows over limestone, which creates more favorable conditions for the tiny insects and other creatures that the trout eat. The bottom line is that the trout here have more food, so they grow larger.

Little River (good for rainbow trout, brown trout, and bass; see the chapter on scenic drives) is the most popular stream in the park for fishing, partly because it's so easy to reach by car. In fact, it's among *Trout Unlimited*'s top 100 trout streams in America. The Sinks (between Metcalf Bottoms Picnic Area and the Townsend "Y") offers deep pools and the largest waterfall on the river. (A local fisherman caught a legendary 29-inch brown here!) Do be careful of the jagged rocks by the falls. Metcalf Bottoms also has good fishing, although it can get crowded with picnickers at lunchtime.

Deep Creek (good for rainbow trout, brown trout, and brook trout) is the only stream in the park where browns outnumber rainbows (although they're harder to catch). Perhaps the easiest place here for families to fish is in the Deep Creek Campground or just upstream from here, except in the summer when it's crowded with tubers. Then, try Indian Creek (see the chapter on waterfall hikes), the first major tributary, about a mile upstream from the campground.

Lower Abrams Creek (good for rainbow trout and bass) in Cades Cove is the best place in the park to hook large rainbows. You can sometimes see river otters here, too. Fish the creek near the trailhead for the Abrams Falls Trail (five miles roundtrip; see the chapter on waterfall hikes) as well as along the trail itself. Another good place is around the relatively remote Abrams Creek Campground.

Cataloochee Creek (good for rainbow and brook trout) is another place where large browns predominate, although they're not as easy to catch as the rainbows. A good spot for families to fish here is around the Cataloochee Campground, which sits right on the creek.

Bradley Fork (good for rainbow trout and brown trout) flows right through Smokemont Campground (see the chapter on camping), just

FUN fact

The park is home to four federally protected fish species and they all live in lower Abrams Creek: the spotfin chub and yellowfin madtom (both considered threatened) and the duskytail darter and smoky madtom (both endangered).

Fishing at Deep Creek.

before joining the Oconaluftee River. The campground is a great fishing spot. You can also catch brook trout in the higher parts of this stream.

Cosby Creek (rainbow and brook trout) flows through Cosby Campground (closed in winter; see the chapter on camping). Anywhere along the road to the campground can be a great spot for family fishing.

The Middle Prong of the Little River (rainbow trout, brown trout, and brook trout) is famous for its very large browns. The upper graveled portion of the Tremont Road (off of Laurel Creek Road near the Townsend "Y") is an excellent spot to fish and quite easy to get to.

Check out the fishing at Gatlinburg's Herbert Holt Park and Mynatt Park, both of which are famous as kids-only fishing zones (restricted to anglers ages 12 and younger), with no license required. The odds are pretty good here, because the town of Gatlinburg stocks its rivers with eight- to 14-inch rainbow trout every Thursday (tossing in up to 45,000 fish per year). The rainbows come from a city hatchery located right at Holt Park. Stocking day is a no-fishing day, making Fridays the best days to fish. As in the national park, you can't use live bait here.

FISHING TIPS

The following fishing tips come from the book *Great Smoky Mountains National Park Angler's Companion* by Ian Rutter, a longtime Smoky Mountain fisherman who is a partner in a Townsend fly-fishing guide service.

• For fly-fishermen, an eight-foot, four-weight rod is the best universal fishing rod to use in the Smokies.

• Long casts are difficult here, so use short casts. For fly-fishermen, the norm here is leaders that are 7.5 feet or shorter.

• Because of all the vegetation in the park, it's best to use sidearm casts rather than overhead casts to keep your flies out of the trees.

• Avoid wearing bright colors so you won't stand out against the background, making you more easily visible to the fish.

• You'll probably have better luck in swifter water and little pools than deep pools because you are less obvious to the fish.

• Stay low, move slowly, face upstream, and avoid wading if you can so you won't spook the fish. And don't let your shadow fall on the water.

• Fish a spot for a short while and then move on. Don't stay in one place too long.

• In winter, you'll catch more fish on mild days than cold ones. For the same reason, fishing where there's more sunlight is better (and will keep you warmer, too). The best time to fish in winter is from 11 a.m. until 3 p.m.

• In spring, the best fishing is during colder days after a spell of mild weather. As the weather warms up, the fishing will be good well into the evening.

• In summer, the fishing is often best after a brief storm. In addition, the larger streams fish best early in the morning or late in the evening.

• Fall is probably the worst season for fishing—but it doesn't mean you won't have fun or get lucky.

CHAPTER 17

Best Bets Outside the Park

As fabulous a playground as the national park is, the gateway communities surrounding the park also offer some high-quality educational experiences that are downright fun by any kid's standards. Here's a description of some of the best such opportunities outside the park's boundaries. (Call ahead to confirm hours, which are subject to change, and for current prices; also ask about available discounts.)

Rainforest Adventures
Sevierville, TN

Are your kids clamoring to be tickled by a tarantula? Would they perhaps prefer to pet an African crested porcupine? Either way, you won't find these creatures in the national park, but you *will* find them living nearby in fancy indoor digs at Rainforest Adventures. This Sevierville attraction, themed by a zoological contractor who worked on Disney World's Animal Kingdom, showcases more than 400 animals belonging to more than 130 species from rainforests around the world.

As you're looking at the lemurs from Madagascar and pondering the poison dart frogs from Costa Rica, be sure to check out the display about the Smokies (which does, after all, contain a high-altitude rainforest; see the chapter on hikes with a view).

Here, you can read about several notable species, including the park's famous flashers (the **fireflies** that light up in unison here during the summer; see the chapter on animals) and the Smokies' celebrity **salamanders**. One interactive exhibit allows you to guess which group of animals (insects, mammals, birds, amphibians, or reptiles) has the most species in the Smokies. Another lets you page through notebooks from field botanists and read their stories about collecting and typing all the life forms in the park.

Address: 280 Collier Dr., Sevierville, TN 37862

Phone: 1-865-428-4091

Website: www.rfadventures.com

Hours: Open daily (except Christmas) from 9 a.m. to 5 p.m.

Location: From the Great Smoky Mountains Parkway (U.S. 441) in Sevierville, turn onto Collier Drive at traffic light #13.4, right across the road from Walmart. Rainforest Adventure will be soon on your left.

Outside, you'll find the **Aussie Walkabout**, which exhibits many unusual animals from Down Under (including kangaroos, wallabies and emus).

Be sure to catch the 45-minute **live animal show**, offered at 11 a.m., 1 p.m., and 3 p.m. Encourage your kids to volunteer. They could end up holding some of the animals (none of which bite or are dangerous, including the tarantula and the corn snake).

Great Smoky Mountains Heritage Center
Townsend, TN

Learn how to speak Cherokee, see possessions from the famous Walker sisters, and peek into an outhouse at this relatively new center highlighting the cultural heritage of East Tennessee (including both the European settlers and the Native Americans).

Start inside. The film in the **theater** varies; sometimes it's the same as the one shown in the park's Sugarlands Visitor Center (see the chapter on visitor centers).

The **transportation gallery** shows off all sorts of early modes of transport, everything from mules to Model T's.

Head to the main exhibit hall to find **interactive displays** along with a huge collection of intriguing **artifacts**. The first half includes Native American artifacts from the Townsend area, some dating from 5,000 years ago. Videos show people making pottery and projectile points. At one computer station, your kids can type in an English word and then hear the Cherokee translation and see the word written in Cherokee symbols. At another computer station, they can play a game called Chunkey.

The rest of the exhibits highlight the pioneer and mountain culture of the communities scattered around what is now the national park. You can walk through a fully furnished log cabin (complete with hickory broom, spinning wheel, and other items from the Walker sisters' cabin; see the chapter on other family-fun hikes), sit on a church pew, see what a mountain schoolhouse looked like, and listen to mountain music.

Outside, follow the gravel path to tour all of the **historic buildings**, brought here from surrounding counties. In addition to an 1892 log cabin, you can see a smokehouse, two cantilever barns, a gristmill,

Address: 123 Cromwell Dr., Townsend, TN 37882

Phone: 1-865-448-0044

Website: www.gsmheritagecenter.org

Hours: Tuesday through Saturday, 10 a.m. to 5 p.m.; Sunday, 1 p.m. to 5 p.m.; closed Monday

Location: On Highway 321, 0.8 mile from the park boundary in Townsend.

Great Smoky Mountains Heritage Center in Townsend, TN.

a granary, a wheelwright shop, and even an outhouse (complete with Sears catalogue)!

Townsend is near the Townsend "Y", the entrance to the park closest to Cades Cove.

Museum of the Cherokee Indian
Cherokee, NC

You'll begin your tour of this museum hearing a story about what you might think of as the female Native American counterpart to Spiderman. In a short film, a Cherokee storyteller will recount the tale of how this fragile little insect was able to bring a burning coal across the water after all the larger, stronger animals failed. As a result, the people had fire. Spider power, indeed!

Although you'll see plenty of **ancient artifacts** (like a 200-year-old authentic dugout canoe), many of the exhibits here depicting the Cherokee's 11,000-year history are done with **computer-generated imagery and special effects**, designed in part by Disney imagineers. In a particularly memorable one, a medicine man suddenly appears as if by magic to tell the story of how plants came to be used as medicine. At the Sequoyah exhibit, you can hear each of the Cherokee syllables as their symbols light up on a giant screen.

This museum is also the official interpretive site for the National Park Service's

Address: 589 Tsali Boulevard, Cherokee, NC 28719

Phone: 1-828-497-3481

Website: www.cherokeemuseum.org

Hours: Open daily from 9 a.m. to 5 p.m. (in the summer, until 7 p.m. every day but Sunday), except Thanksgiving, Christmas, and New Year's Day.

Location: At U.S. 441 and Tsali Boulevard

Trail of Tears National Historic Trail. A poignant series of exhibits relates the heartbreaking story of how in 1838, the U.S. government forced more than 15,000 Cherokees to leave their ancestral home and walk more than a thousand miles to what is now Oklahoma. Almost half of the tribe died along the way. See the 160-year-old gun used to execute Tsali, a Cherokee farmer who resisted leaving. His descendants are among the Cherokee who remained, who today make up the Eastern Band of the Cherokee.

Cherokee, NC, is just a few miles from the Oconaluftee entrance to the park, including the Oconaluftee Visitor Center (see the chapter on visitor centers), the Mountain Farm Museum (see the chapter on self-guiding nature trails), and the trailhead for the Oconaluftee River Trail.

In Cherokee, there is no word for "goodbye." The Cherokee phrase used instead translates as "Until we meet again."

Oconaluftee Village
Cherokee, NC; closed in winter

Instead of imagining what it would be like to live in a Cherokee village, your family can actually walk through one, watching as the women weave colorful cloth, bead beautiful belts, turn river cane into baskets, and coil clay to fashion pots used for cooking and storage. The men chip away at flint to make arrowheads or carve pieces of wood or soapstone to make both utilitarian and ceremonial objects. Others fashion blowguns for hunting and practice their aim (at a target, not their guests). Another man uses fire to burn out the middle of what will eventually become a dugout canoe.

The Oconaluftee Village is a re-creation of a Cherokee community from about 1750. As you tour the village with your guide (or wander through on your own after your tour), you can watch the Cherokees as they work and ask them questions. During certain times you can even **sign up for classes** taught by village artisans and make your own Cherokee crafts using techniques that are thousands of years old.

Address: P.O. Box 398, Cherokee, NC 28719

Phone: 1-866-554-4557 or 1-828-497-2111

Website: www.cherokee-nc.com

Hours: Open every day from 9:00 a.m. to 5:30 p.m., from early May through mid-October

Location: Drama Road beside the Mountainside Theatre

Compare the **three historic cabins**, one from the 1500s, one from the 1700s, and one from the 1800s. (Despite the stereotype, the Cherokee did not live in teepees.) Learn the difference between the sweat house, used for medicinal purposes, and the sweat lodge, used for spiritual ceremonies.

In the seven-sided **Council House**, learn about the seven clans (each of which has its own job) and how the tribe was governed from this

Oconaluftee Village in Cherokee, NC.

building. You'll also see the elaborate headdresses and beautiful feather capes worn for special occasions by certain important people.

In the sacred **Square Grounds**, you'll learn why this holy spot is considered the soul of the village and about the Cherokees' sacred ceremonies. You may even get to see an example of ceremonial dancing.

Just outside the village is the winding, idyllic **Botanical Trail** (free to the public) where 150 or so of the more than 800 indigenous plants and herbs the Cherokee traditionally used bear labels telling you what their use was. (The inner bark of the wild hydrangeas *stops* vomiting, for example, while the outer bark *induces* vomiting.) Cherokee elders and other storytellers sometimes sit in special spots along the walk, sharing stories from their culture.

As you wander through this mile-long trail, listen for frogs, look for spider webs catching the morning dew, hop across streamlets on rocks or over them on bridges, and smell the smoke from the fires of the Oconaluftee Village next door.

In the Cherokee tribe, the women were the heads of the clans and had important roles in governing the tribe. Men would go to live with their wives' clans when they got married, although they always remained members of their own original clan.

The outdoor drama Unto These Hills is the longest-running outdoor drama in the U.S. Recently rewritten and completely updated, the now shares a culturally authentic and historically accurate view of the history of the Cherokees, from their creation myth through the Trail of Tears and to the present day. (Monday through Saturday, 7:00 p.m., from mid-June through August; 866-554-4557; www.cherokee-nc.com.)

AFTER YOUR VISIT

After your go back home, help your kids pick some activities that will encourage them to remember their time at Great Smoky Mountains National Park. Below are some suggestions. See if you can come up with other ideas.

Write a letter: Have each of your kids write a note to the Park Service telling the rangers a story about something they saw or did in the park that they will never forget. Maybe they will want to write about seeing a bear, going camping for the first time, hiking on their favorite trail, or even participating in a really fun ranger program. Encourage them to include at least one new thing that they learned on their trip.

Mail the letters to: Great Smoky Mountains National Park, 107 Park Headquarters Road, Gatlinburg, TN 37738.

Draw a picture: Have your kids draw pictures of their favorite moments in the park. If they're old enough, have them write captions for the pictures that include whatever information they think is significant about the experience they drew. If they're too young to write the captions themselves, have them dictate captions for each picture so you can write them down.

Consider framing their pictures as souvenirs of your trip or making a scrapbook out of them. If you make a scrapbook, you can also include your own photos, a park map, or other reminders of your trip.

Read a story: Read a story about the park or a park animal from a book that you purchased in one of the park bookstores. (If you didn't have a chance to buy any books while you were visiting the park, you can order some online from the Great Smoky Mountains Association at www.SmokiesInformation.org; every purchase benefits the park.)

Have older children read the story to you or to their younger siblings. Talk about what you recognize in the story that you remember from your trip.

Write a story or act out a play: Have your kids make up an adventure story about a person they met (like a ranger) or an animal they saw while they were visiting the park. Have them incorporate as many place names as they can remember from the park in their story. See if they can include some things they learned, as well. For example, if they're writing a story about a bear, see if they can remember where bears live and what they eat and include that in the story somehow.

If they're too young to write their story down, suggest that they act out their story using stuffed animals, puppets, or other toys you may have bought for them in one of the park's giftshops. Or you can make your own puppets by having the kids draw pictures of their characters and then cutting them out and gluing them onto pieces of cardboard. (Attach cardboard strips to the back of the pictures for handles to make using the puppets easier.)

Watch a video: Watch a video or DVD together about the park or about one or more of the animals you saw while you were there. Talk about what was in the video that you remembered from your visit, and also talk about what new things you learned from watching it.

Do a park puzzle: Make a large print of one of your favorite pictures of the Smokies (maybe even one including your family members having fun in the park) and then use scissors to cut it into shapes, making a jigsaw-type puzzle. You can make the puzzle as easy or as difficult as you want.

For extra fun, keep the subject of the puzzle a secret and see if your kids can guess what the picture is as they put it together.

Make a virtual visit: Check out the online webcams of the park so you can see what's going on there right now. (There's a list of webcams at the beginning of chapter 1.)

On the page with the webcam of Look Rock, you can also view Look Rock's weather and air quality data. Consider having your kids bookmark this site and keep track of the data periodically, monitoring changes with each season.

Plan your next trip to the Smokies: Have your kids make a list of what they want to see and do the next time they visit the national park. They can use this book to help them with ideas, or they can go online to visit the national park's website at www.nps.gov/grsm. Be sure to use their list as a guide when you return!

GEOGRAPHIC FAMILY-FUN INDEX

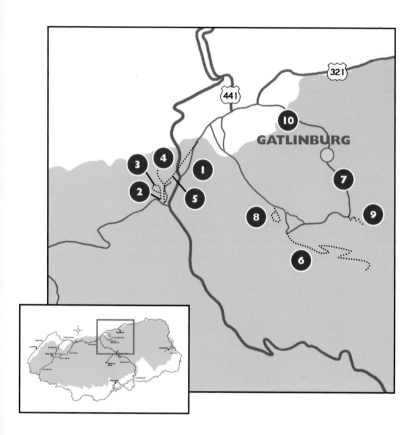

Sugarlands/Gatlinburg area, TN

1. Sugarlands Riding Stables* (Chapter 15)
2. Sugarlands Visitor Center (Chapter 5)
3. Fighting Creek Self-Guiding Nature Trail (Chapter 9)
4. Cataract Falls Trail (Chapter 10) (Y)
5. Gatlinburg Trail (Chapter 12) (Y)
6. Rainbow Falls Trail (Chapter 10)
7. Roaring Fork Motor Nature Trail* (Chapter 6)
8. Noah "Bud" Ogle Self-Guiding Nature Trail (Chapter 9)
9. Grotto Falls Hike* (Chapter 10)
10. Place of a Thousand Drips* (Chapter 10)

closed in winter, or access road to this point is closed in winter
(Y) appropriate for very young hikers

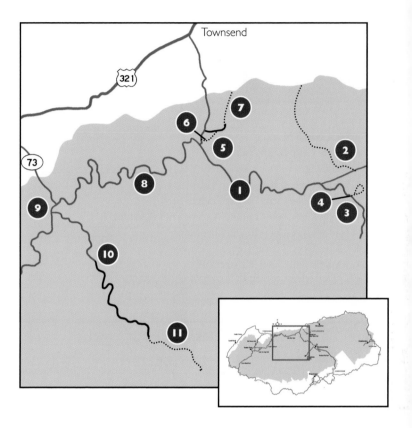

Little River Road, TN

1. Little River Road (Chapter 6)

2. Laurel Falls Self-Guiding Nature Trail (Chapter 10)

3. Elkmont Campground* (Chapter 13)

4. Elkmont Self-Guiding Nature Trail (Chapter 9)

5. Metcalf Bottoms Picnic Area (Chapter 8)

6. Metcalf Bottoms Trail to Little Greenbrier Schoolhouse (Y) (Chapter 12)

7. Little Brier Gap Trail to the Walker sisters' cabin (Chapter 12)

8. Meigs Falls (Chapter 10)

9. Townsend "Y" (Chapter 8)

10. Great Smoky Mountains Institute at Tremont (Chapter 7)

11. Middle Prong Trail to old Cadillac and Indian Flats Falls (Chapter 12)

* closed in winter, or access road to this point is closed in winter

(Y) appropriate for very young hikers

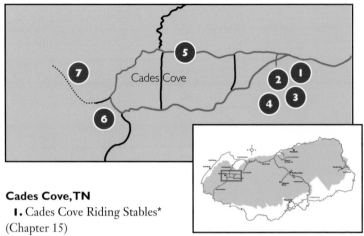

Cades Cove, TN

1. Cades Cove Riding Stables* (Chapter 15)

2. Cades Cove Campground (Chapter 13)

3. Cades Cove Picnic Area (Chapter 8)

4. Cades Cove Self-Guiding Nature Trail (Chapter 9)

5. Cades Cove Loop Road (Chapter 6)

6. Cades Cove Visitor Center (Chapter 5)

7. Abrams Falls Trail (Chapter 10)

closed in winter, or access road to this point is closed in winter

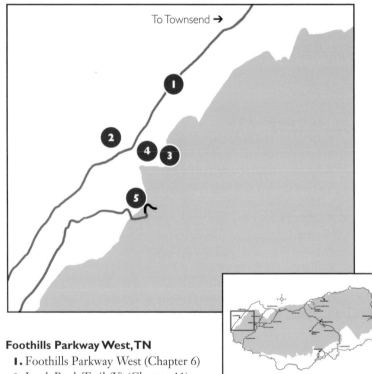

Foothills Parkway West, TN

1. Foothills Parkway West (Chapter 6)

2. Look Rock Trail (Y) (Chapter 11)

3. Look Rock Campground* (Chapter 13)

4. Look Rock Picnic Area* (Chapter 8)

5. Abrams Creek Campground* (Chapter 13)

closed in winter, or access road to this point is closed in winter

(Y) appropriate for very young hikers

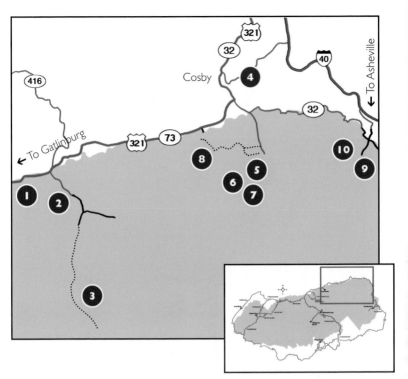

Northern Border of the Park, TN/NC

1. Smoky Mountain Riding Stables* (Chapter 15)
2. Greenbrier Picnic Area (Chapter 8)
3. Porters Creek Trail (Y) (Chapter 12)
4. Foothills Parkway East (Chapter 6)
5. Cosby Campground* (Chapter 13)
6. Cosby Picnic Area (Chapter 8
7. Cosby Self-Guiding Nature Trail (Chapter 9)
8. Hen Wallow Falls Hike (Chapter 10)
9. Big Creek Campground* (Chapter 13)
10. Big Creek Picnic Area (Chapter 8)

closed in winter, or access road to this point is closed in winter

(Y) appropriate for very young hikers

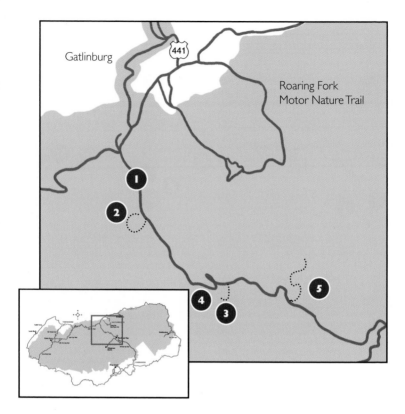

Newfound Gap Road (U.S. 441) in Tennessee
1. Newfound Gap Road (U.S. 441) (Chapter 6)
2. Sugarlands Valley Self-Guiding Nature Trail (Chapter 9)
3. Cove Hardwood Self-Guiding Nature Trail (Chapter 9)
4. Chimneys Picnic Area (Chapter 8)
5. Alum Cave Trail (Chapter 11)

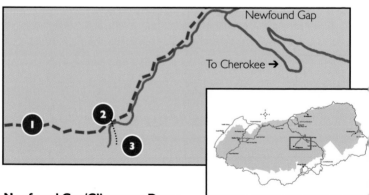

Newfound Gap/Clingmans Dome
1. Appalachian Trail (Chapter 12)
2. Clingmans Dome Self-Guiding Nature Trail* (Chapter 11)
3. Andrews Bald Trail* (Chapter 11)

closed in winter, or access road to this point is closed in winter

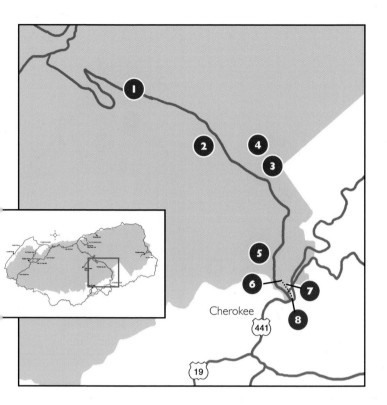

Newfound Gap Road (U.S. 441) in North Carolina

1. Newfound Gap Road (U.S. 441) (Chapter 6)
2. Collins Creek Picnic Area* (Chapter 8)
3. Smokemont Campground (Chapter 13)
4. Smokemont Riding Stables* (Chapter 15)
5. Mingus Mill* (Chapter 9)
6. Oconaluftee Visitor Center (Chapter 5)
7. Mountain Farm Museum Self-Guiding Nature Trail (Chapter 9)
8. Oconaluftee River Trail (Y) (Chapter 12)

closed in winter, or access road to this point is closed in winter

(Y) appropriate for very young hikers

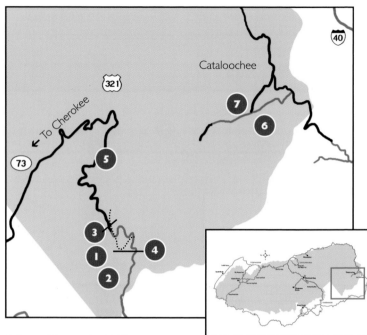

Balsam Mountain, NC*

1. Balsam Mountain Campground* (Chapter 13)
2. Balsam Mountain Self-Guiding Nature Trail* (Chapter 9)
3. Heintooga Picnic Area and Overlook* (Chapter 8)
4. Flat Creek Trail* (Chapter 12)
5. Balsam Mountain Road* (Chapter 6)

closed in winter, or access road to this point is closed in winter

Cataloochee, NC

6. Cataloochee Campground* (Chapter 13)
7. Cataloochee auto tour (Chapter 6)

closed in winter, or access road to this point is closed in winter

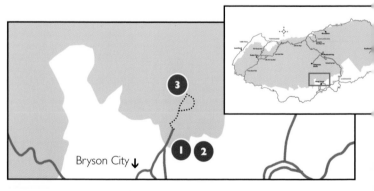

Deep Creek, NC

1. Deep Creek Campground* (Chapter 13)
2. Deep Creek Picnic Area (Chapter 8)
3. Three Waterfalls Loop hike (portions Y) (Chapter 10)

closed in winter, or access road to this point is closed in winter
(Y) appropriate for very young hikers

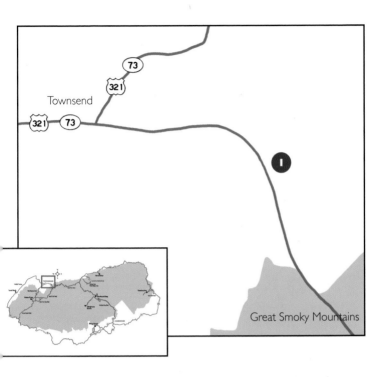

OUTSIDE THE PARK
Townsend, TN
1. Great Smoky Mountains Heritage Center in Townsend (Chapter 17)

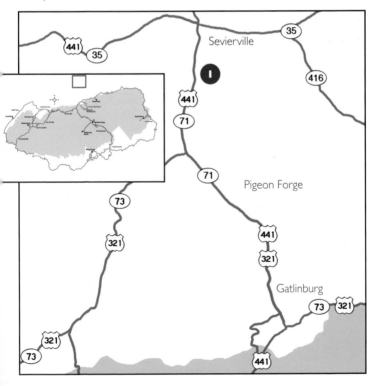

Sevierville, TN
1. Rainforest Adventure (Chapter 17)

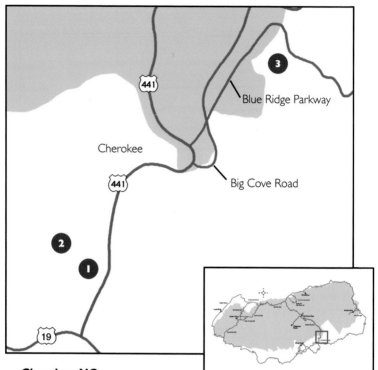

Cherokee, NC
- **1.** Museum of the Cherokee Indian in Cherokee (Chapter 17)
- **2.** Oconaluftee Village* (Chapter 17)
- **3.** Mingo Falls (Chapter 10)

closed in winter, or access road to this point is closed in winter

INDEX